Through his skillful introductions and summaries of ten Catholic classics, D'Souza prepares the reader for an intellectual banquet that can last a lifetime. Though obviously writing after considerable research, D'Souza never permits his scholarship to get in the way of a direct, crisp style which makes the volume a delight to read.

> *JUDE P. DOUGHERTY*
> Dean, School of Philosophy
> Catholic University

For those of us who know the richness of the Catholic tradition and the poverty of our no longer being exposed to these Catholic classics, Dinesh D'Souza's book is most welcome. No book will substitute for reading the classics themselves, but this book will give us an incentive to try, or if we have already read them, to read them again.

> *JAMES V. SCHALL, S.J.*
> Department of Government
> Georgetown University

Dinesh D'Souza's book is a well-written, engaging work providing popular introductions and summaries of classics in Christian literature.

> *WILLIAM MAY*
> Professor of Moral Theology
> Catholic University

D'Souza's chapter on Saint Augustine's *Confessions* is vivid and moving. It will make the reader thirst to read the original and no summary can receive higher praise.

> *JAMES HITCHCOCK*
> Professor of History
> University of Saint Louis

Dinesh D'Souza has done a remarkable job of popularizing without trivializing Thomas Aquinas. It is a standing joke among Thomists that the *Summa* was composed for beginners. D'Souza has done much to bring the work into the reach of those for whom it was intended. All proportion guarded, I feel confident in saying that this summary stands with G.K. Chesterton's great work on Aquinas.

> *RALPH McINERNY*
> Professor of Philosophy
> University of Notre Dame

The Imitation of Christ stands in need of no recommendation from any Christian believer. Dinesh D'Souza's commentary gives a balanced and enlightening introduction for both old friends of the *Imitation* and those who come to it for the first time.

Dinesh D'Souza's chapter on Boethius's *Consolation of Philosophy* is an excellent piece of work, high-level popularization at its best. It is an accurate, clear, interesting, illuminating, and inspiring work. It takes great skill to write like this.

I was particularly impressed with D'Souza's eloquent chapter on Dante. He shows us Dante the poet as only Dante himself could do better. The chapter is an invitation to flight — to the heart of love.

This remarkable book — a synthesis of biographic detail and substantive analysis — will encourage all readers to reflect on these classics and to read them in their entirety. It will promote the process of "faith seeking understanding."

Possessed of a talent for making lucid concepts that have often seemed obscure, D'Souza gives us the essence of the meaning of Catholic literature down the centuries. In a time when the Catholic intellect seems impoverished in the United States, *The Catholic Classics* is a book to wake us to the genius of what has been, and what may be again.

the Catholic Classics

Dinesh D'Souza

Introductory Comments by
Cardinal John J. O'Connor and William F. Buckley, Jr.

Our Sunday Visitor Publishing Division
Our Sunday Visitor, Inc.
Huntington, Indiana 46750

Acknowledgments

Scripture texts contained in this work are taken from the *Revised Standard Version Bible, Catholic Edition,* © 1965 and 1966 by the Division of Christian Education of the National Council of the Churches of Christ in the U.S.A., and used by permission of the copyright owner. Other sources from which material has been excerpted or has served (either quoted verbatim or paraphrased) as the basis for portions of this work include standard versions of the various Catholic classics, among them *Apologia Pro Vita Sua,* © 1968 by W.W. Norton & Co., Inc., New York, N.Y.; *Imitation of Christ,* © 1955 by Doubleday & Co., Inc., Garden City, N.Y.; and *Seven Storey Mountain,* © 1948 by Harcourt Brace Jovanovich, Inc., New York, N.Y. If any copyrighted materials have been inadvertently used in this book without proper credit being given, please notify Our Sunday Visitor in writing so that future printings of this work may be corrected accordingly.

International Standard Book Number: 0-87973-545-7
Library of Congress Catalog Card Number: 86-61500

Cover design by James E. McIlrath

PRINTED IN THE UNITED STATES OF AMERICA

For my parents,
Allan and Margaret D'Souza

CONTENTS

preface

IT was in the late 1930s, as memory serves me, and on through the 1940s that books like *The Catholic Classics* were appearing one after the other, and exciting a generation thirsting for precisely the kind of excitement they offered. Dominican Father Thomas Farrell's book *Companion to the Summa* uniquely revealed the very special beauty of the interweaving of the spiritual and the intellectual in the *Summa Theologica*. So appealing was Father Farrell's book that spiritual directors were soon referring their charges in large numbers to a pocket-size condensation of it, called *My Way of Life*. I am not sure that those of us who were priests in that day fully appreciated the reality that many, many laymen were thus reading Thomas Aquinas with perhaps more spiritual benefit than some of us had derived when studying the original.

New editions of G.K. Chesterton began to proliferate at the time, side by side with portable Cardinal Newmans. Publishers Frank Sheed and Maisie Ward were becoming household names. Hilaire Belloc, Paul Claudel, François Mauriac, Léon Bloy, Georges Bernanos, Evelyn Waugh, Eric Gill and even, for the more mystically oriented, Gerard Manley Hopkins — all became known, all evoked to a greater or lesser degree some sense of what Frank O'Malley called "the integrating power of a real faith and truth." It is small wonder that Thomas Merton's *Seven Storey Mountain* was an instant success; countless numbers of readers had already been prepared by such as the above to recognize why Merton's search would lead to his conversion.

It was at least the *hope* of a spiritual renascence that we were experiencing in those days, perhaps nowhere so winsomely portrayed as in Myles Connolly's *Mr. Blue*, a little Catholic classic itself, that must have broken all sales records of its day. Indeed, it would in no way demean Dinesh D'Souza's *The Catholic Classics* to observe that the reprinting of *Mr. Blue* and its reappearance in bookstores these many years later suggests that the world is ready again for the excitement D'Souza's work generates. Chesterton is back, as well, in a variety of popular formats, as are brand-new editions of Thomas à Kempis. The time is indeed opportune.

Dinesh D'Souza's skill in revealing the essence of each of the classics he synthesizes (as well as the personality of the author who produced it) is quite reminiscent of Father Farrell's and that alone, I wager, will guarantee a reading. More significantly, I suspect that the author has accurately gauged the new thirst and turned wisely to the wellspring that he calls *The Catholic Classics*, to show us how the thirst can be quenched. Each of his selections is, indeed, a classic. Each is "traditionally" Catholic, which is to say quite the opposite of its being therefore "pre-Vatican II" or "pre-Trent."

There is a dynamic orthodoxy that pulsates and radiates through each of the works synthesized here, as well as through the life of each author. To be introduced to both the works and the authors for the first time, or to be reintroduced to old friends, is to be in touch with what Saint Augustine called "beauty ever ancient, ever new." But more, it's to come upon an ice-cold spring and to be startled by the sweetness that reveals how jaded one's taste may have become.

Not a few Catholics weary of *ersatz* Catholicism will be refreshed by *The Catholic Classics*. Many *not* of our faith will be quietly gladdened to have available this recollection of what we once believed, and still believe.

John Cardinal O'Connor
ARCHBISHOP OF NEW YORK

introduction

ON the day I sat down to write this introduction the New York *Times* carried a few letters from Catholics reacting to a piece that had appeared a week or so earlier by a woman who styled herself a "cultural Catholic." She meant by this (she had explained) that in a palpable but inexplicable way she continued to think of herself as a Catholic. Thus was she baptized, as such married; and, in due course, she expected that she would be buried under the sign of the Cross. But that was about it, save possibly for church attendance on Christmas and Easter.

The reaction included a letter from a laicized priest who remarked his own familiarity with her type and recounted an experience he had had shortly before his resignation. A man brought in a child to be baptized, after which ceremony he said cheerfully to the priest, "Well, Father, that's probably the last time you'll see me in church." Apparently it was episodes such as these, much multiplied, that caused the priest to incline to secular pursuits. He reports now that he is married, and that his wife is expecting a child.

Such stories are most awfully depressing, and one needs to recall other historical periods marked by religious indifference to remind oneself that there is no reason to expect that we live in a unique season, in which the faith is dying all over the world. There have always been jeremiads to that effect. To be sure, there is something about our own period that gives them an acute meaning; I mean the capacity, developed during the twentieth century, on the one hand to acquire near-ultimate sophistication in the techniques of oppression, on the other, the century's introduction of apocalyptic weapons.

What Dinesh D'Souza's remarkable volume does for us is sharply to remind us of the most neglected patrimony in civilization, which is the exegesis of the great minds that devoted themselves as feverishly as any prospector looking for gold to searching out the meaning of God, and the role of Christ, mediator. We live, in America, in a society relatively careless about physical health, but even so there are fifty million ex-cigarette smokers in our midst. Whereas we know of at least one priest informed by a father bringing his son there for baptism that that was the father's terminal experience in church, it is unlikely one can find one doctor who has had the experience of a mother bringing in an infant for an injection who thereafter announced that that was the last time any doctor would minister to her child.

We have seen, in America, a generation of young people aware of biological data ignored by their parents, many of them at mortal consequence, having to do not only with cigarettes, but with obesity, with the failure to exercise, with alcohol, with cholesterol. For these there are spiritual counterparts: we are a nation disposed to cultural Christianity. We are a nation whose allegiance to religion is a lackadaisical habit. Baptisms, Easter services, marriages, and funerals are fixed mortgage-pay-ment rendezvous; theology is the fine print, to be stared at by a remote monk, and here and there a theology professor.

What Dinesh D'Souza has done is to magnify that fine print, reword it as required, give it a historic and philosophical narrative, and lo! it leaps to life, and we are reminded that there are very grave reasons why man's ancestors, and now his progeny, submit to baptism. We are introduced — in some cases, reintroduced — to divisions within Christian thought that sundered whole nations, affecting western history, western thought, philosophy, literature, poetry. It is D'Souza's implied contention (he is never, in this volume, either didactic, impatient, or remonstrative) that a mere exposure to the bony extra-biblical tissue of Christian thinking is at least worth the reading time; at most, it can change the reader's vision of the meaning of life.

D'Souza's plan is at once workaday, and ingenious. Rather than attempt a historical narrative of Catholic theology, he takes individuals who are large in Catholic thought and literature and tells us about them: about the times they lived in, the matters that engrossed them, the contributions they made. Boethius can be read as a great classical scholar — "the last Roman philosopher, the first medieval scholastic." But his concern for philosophy was rooted in his concern for man: "Eternity is the whole and perfect possession of unlimited life at once."

The Venerable Bede tells us, more clearly than anyone else, how it was that the Christian religion colonized the western world. A figure, in life, perhaps exemplary to the point of incredulity. . . . How is this for a deathbed scene: "As his energy began to leave his body, Bede summoned the priests, who said Mass for him and gave him the last sacraments. After this the boy [his amanuensis],

12

nervous and afraid, blurted out, 'Sir, there is still a sentence which is not written down.' Bede replied, 'Well, then go ahead and write it.' When the boy said, 'It is finished,' Bede sat back and said, 'You have said the truth. It is finished.' He sang the Gloria Patri and died." Compare Ronald Knox who, on *his* deathbed, asked if he would like to be read to from his own translation of the Bible, answered, Hell no. This isn't impiety speaking, it is man, finally demonstrating that he is not an angel.

D'Souza reminds us that although Thomas Aquinas believed that the fact of God could be demonstrated, he nevertheless acknowledged that the truth about Him, arrived by reason, could be apprehended "only by a very few men, and after a long time, and with the admixture of many errors." Even so, Aquinas himself was eminently understandable, anxious always to remove any poetic lint from his prose, the better to enhance lucidity. Dante is known in the secular world as a poet, and so it is refreshing to be reminded of the seriousness with which he undertook what he understood as a divine mandate, in language pehaps unequaled in any other tongue, to produce his divine comedy.

D'Souza gives a fine brief overview of Blaise Pascal, about whom it is widely supposed that he was a Christian only in the stop-loss sense that investors arrange with their brokers. But his faith was deep, notwithstanding his belief that "truth lies beyond our scope and is an unattainable quarry," the two derivative excesses being to exclude reason, and to admit nothing but reason. One has to get seriously into the discipline if one hopes to come anywhere near to the imitation of Christ. But Thomas à Kempis, spiritual perfectionist, scorned the superficial spiritual modus vivendi — "Jesus has many lovers of his kingdom, but he has few bearers of his cross."

We reach John Henry Newman, the most elegant and belletristic Catholic apologist of the nineteenth century, a profound scholar of refined sensibilities who agonized over his ineluctable passage to Rome, and then pronounced it triumphantly gratifying. You see, "dogma has been the fundamental principle of my religion. I know no other religion. I cannot enter into the idea of any other sort of religion. Religion, as mere sentiment, is to me a dream and a mockery." And, to conclude, a chapter on Chesterton, and on Thomas Merton. Every time one reads Chesterton, or about Chesterton, one is surprised by how he continues to surprise. Thomas Merton, D'Souza in effect acknowledges, is not a fixed figure either in the evolution of Christian theology or Christian manners; but as a contemporary he is an arresting figure, the man who, in the affluent society, turned to the Cistercian order.

These are the men Dinesh D'Souza celebrates in his introductory volume to great Catholic thinkers, to remind us of the profound and imaginative minds that, with the help of God, have sustained the Christian religion through the deserts of neglect. His purpose is to quicken the religious fancy of the reader, not by catechetical immersion, not by devotional exercises, but by a quiet examination of the excitement of theological thought. Those touched by his work will be grateful to him, as they are drawn closer to Him.

William F. Buckley, Jr.

O · N · E

augustine's

confessions

SAINT Augustine's *Confessions* is a painfully candid and eloquent account of the author's conversion to Christianity. Written around A.D. 397, the *Confessions* had a profound influence not only on the early Middle Ages but also on later medieval thinkers such as Saints Anselm, Bonaventure, and Thomas Aquinas. Perhaps no work other than the Bible had a greater impact on early Christian culture. The *Confessions* is also one of the first autobiographical works that has survived to the present day.

The historical importance of Saint Augustine is that he stood at the junction between the old pagan world and the new Christian culture that was supplanting it. Using philosophical concepts of the Greek philosopher Plato, Augustine was able to "baptize" or transform them to suit Christian doctrine. Thus, Augustine provided a bridge between Greco-Roman ideas and Christian doctrine. In the *Confessions* Augustine vividly describes how he himself made the transition from Neoplatonism to orthodox Catholicism.

The *Confessions* makes fairly difficult reading because it is written in an ornate Latin style whose sentences never seem to end. To the impatient reader, perusing Augustine is like moving very slowly through a revolving door. Besides, Augustine frequently interrupts his narrative with passionate praise for God's greatness and compassion. Yet, for all that, the *Confessions* rewards the persistent reader, because it draws him or her into the depths of Augustine's soul and, almost miraculously, into the depths of the reader's own soul. In other words, the *Confessions* rises above the circumstances of its time — ultimately it is a book about the naked soul standing before its Maker.

To the modern reader, Augustine's self-incrimination for his sins seems a bit excessive. He is constantly beating his breast over a petty theft during his childhood or for taking a mistress. Although we do not condone stealing or engaging in illicit sexual activity, such things are commonplace in our time, and we have a hard time getting worked up about them. But does that reflect something about Augustine or about ourselves? The value of the *Confessions* today is that it illuminates the meaning and omnipresence of sin when so many of us have ceased to take it seriously. Watching Augustine agonize over his lust and avarice, we are tempted to sneer at his lack of sophistication or chuckle at his righteousness, and yet there is a strange glimmer in our souls — the glimmer of recognition of the fall of man, of our own sins, of our need for redemption, and of the saving grace of Jesus Christ.

Augustine was born in the year 354 in a small town called Tagaste in north Africa, in what is now Algeria. His father was a minor Roman official and a pagan, but his mother, Monica, was a fervent Christian whose love pursued Augustine down the lanes of his sinful life, and no matter how fast he ran he could not escape her maternal love and concern. She is a central character in the

Confessions, because even when she is not physically present she is a presence; her heartfelt prayers for her wayward son constantly tug at his proud mind and his hardened heart. "Achilles absent, was Achilles still," Homer writes in the *Iliad*. So it is with Monica, and it is right that the *Confessions* opens with her attachment to her newborn son, and ends with her death following Augustine's conversion and reconciliation with her.

The first striking section in the *Confessions* is Augustine's brilliant and shocking account of the evils perpetrated by babies. Infants strike us as gurgling and innocent, he says, and yet they demand constant attention; cry whenever something is denied them, including things that would harm them; envy their brother's and sister's toys and mother's milk; throw tantrums and kick nurses who refuse to pander to them. "If babies are innocent," Augustine writes, "it is not for lack of will to do harm, but for lack of strength." This is an insightful if not wholly convincing attempt to demonstrate original sin.

In his childhood Augustine learned the rudiments of Greek, which he hated, and Latin, which he liked. He became attached to the novel and tragic tales of the Trojan War and the wanderings of Aeneas. Yet after his conversion he developed a distaste for these "fictions," because they distracted him from his own failings. "I was obliged to memorize the adventures of Aeneas, while in the meantime I forgot my own erratic ways," Augustine writes. "I lamented the death of Dido, who killed herself for love, while in the midst of this I was dying, separated from you, my God and my Life, and I shed no tears for my own plight."

Augustine seems to take an entirely negative view of secular poetry, theater, and music, because — as he points out — they inflame the wrong passions. It would serve us well to keep some of his cautions in mind, since many movies and television programs regularly glamorize cruelty, crime, lust, and greed. Augustine raises the question, "Why do men enjoy feeling sad at the sight of cruelty and suffering on the stage, even though they would be most unhappy if they had to endure the same fate themselves?" He suggests that "we enjoy pitying others, and we welcome their misfortunes, without which we could not pity them." Yet Augustine says he feels greater pity for men who are happy in their sins than for those who forgo some pleasure "which was really an affliction."

In 370, at the age of sixteen, Augustine went to Carthage (in modern-day Tunisia), where he began the study of rhetoric. There he writes, "The brambles of lust grew high above my head and there was no one to root them out," not even his father, who found his concupiscence highly amusing. His mother warned him not to fornicate, and most of all not to seduce other men's wives, but Augustine found this "womanish advice." The magnitude of Augustine's lust embarrasses the devout Christian reader of the *Confessions*; it undermines the notion of the saint as some sort of timid ascetic, completely indifferent to the attractions of this world, his soul riveted on the next.

Besides well-formed women, Augustine also coveted material possessions, often just for the sake of acquiring them. In one of the most famous incidents in his *Confessions*, Augustine and some friends steal pears from a neighbor's tree. But this was no boyish prank, Augustine assures us; it was an insidious evil, because his parents had a pear tree at home overloaded with fruit, and "I had no wish to enjoy the things I stole, but only to enjoy the theft itself and the sin." So this, Augustine tells us, was evil for its own sake, the most direct defiance of the God who made us in his own image.

"You have made us for yourself, and our hearts are without rest until they find rest in you," writes Augustine in the best-known line in the book. But he still has many miles to go before he sleeps. In Carthage he is caught up in the licentious ways of the great port. He revels in the obscene rites connected with Eastern religions, the chants and belly-wiggling; unable to contain his lust, Augustine takes a mistress whom he chose "for no special reason but that my passions alighted on her." He lives with this woman for ten years and has a son by her, whom he names Adeodatus.

No less restive than his manhood is his fertile intellect. Augustine finds himself dissatisfied with the Christian doctrines he acquired as a catechumen. He finds Christian rhetoric clumsy compared to the burnished oratory of Cicero, and he believes that Christianity cannot explain "the problem of evil": how a supposedly all-knowing and all-compassionate God could create sin and suffering. After all, if God did not cause these, then where did they come from, since the world was created out of nothing by God alone?

An answer to the problem of evil was suggested by a heretical doctrine called Manicheanism, which in Augustine's time had a great following. According to the Manicheans, there are two absolute principles: a good principle and an evil principle, which are in eternal conflict. In man the soul is composed of light, the good principle, while the body is evil. The Manicheans saw the human struggle as one between mind and body, between spirit and the senses. Perhaps the fact that Augustine found himself unable to control his body was partly the reason

19

he found a doctrine such as Manicheanism so appealing.

His mother, conscious of his sins of the mind and the senses, fasted and prayed for Augustine. She even implored a local bishop to talk to Augustine and refute his errors. But the bishop wisely refrained, remarking that it was not the right time; Augustine was "brimming with the novelty of his heresy," and it was better to leave him alone until God was ready to deal with him. "Don't worry," the bishop told Monica, "the son of so many tears cannot be lost."

A few years later, Augustine was already beginning to be troubled by contradictions in Manicheanism. First, he wondered why there was a necessary conflict between the evil and good principles within man. Why couldn't the soul, he asked, simply refuse to do battle with evil? If the Manicheans replied that avoiding battle could result in the evil force harming the good force, then they conceded that the good force was subject to hurt and corruption, which was impossible, since it was created by God and of the same substance as the Creator. On the other hand, if the Manicheans maintained that the evil force posed no threat to the good force, then there would be no purpose in engaging it in battle.

Another point which disturbed Augustine was that Manichean dualism did not seem to correspond to actual conflicts in the world. For example, if a man is deciding whether to commit murder by poison or murder by stabbing, it is difficult to maintain that either of these is inspired by the good force. Besides, there may be more than two choices — perhaps the murderer also wants to rob the house and rape his victim's wife. This profusion of possibilities, Augustine reasoned, could not be reconciled with simplistic divisions of everything into absolute good and absolute evil.

Returning to teach in his hometown of Tagaste, Augustine made a very close friend who shared his intelligence and contempt for things unexplained. Their relationship was "sweeter than all the joys of life I explored before then," Augustine writes, but suddenly his friend became very sick and was about to die. The sacraments were administered by his family; then he miraculously recovered. Augustine rushed to his side and made cruel jokes about his baptism. He expected his friend to repudiate the sacrament now that he was well. Instead the young man looked at Augustine in horror "as though I were an enemy." Shocked, Augustine withdrew from his presence. A few days later the boy had a relapse and died. Later Augustine would thank God he had not succeeded in convincing his friend to reject the Christian faith, but at the time he felt only numbing grief, which added to his intellectual uncertainty.

The Manicheans assured Augustine that all his dilemmas would be resolved by Faustus, their noted bishop, who was scheduled to speak in the area. Augustine found him cheerful and articulate, but unable to meet his objections, and even willing to admit his ignorance. Disappointed, Augustine abandoned his Manichean views and left for Rome to teach rhetoric at a school there. About a year later he went to Milan where he continued teaching rhetoric.

In Milan he agreed to marry the woman of his mother's choice, but she was not yet the legal age, and "I could not possibly endure the life of a celibate," Augustine writes. His mistress had left him and returned to Africa, so rather than wait for two years to be married, Augustine took a second concubine. Feeling guilty about this, he prayed, "Make me chaste, O Lord, but not yet."

Besides swapping mistresses in Milan, Augustine

also swapped philosophies. He dabbled in Neoplatonism, which held that the things of this world are mere replications of noncorporeal ideas. For instance, what we call a "chair" is merely a material representation of the idea of a chair. Where were these ideas? On this point, the Neoplatonists were not too specific; they were out in the heavens somewhere, they said. What was attractive about Neoplatonism was that it transcended materialism; it held that there were abstract ideas superior to concrete objects. For Augustine, who previously could not even conceive of immaterial things, Neoplatonism helped him understand the concept of spiritual beings, of a God who was not made of matter but was Existence itself.

Neoplatonism helped Augustine overcome his crucial objection to Christianity. He had wondered how a benevolent God could create evil. But now he understood that there was no such "thing" as evil; contrary to what the Manicheans maintained, there was no evil of itself; rather evil was simply the "absence of due good." So God's creation was indeed, as the Bible says, good in the eyes of the Lord, and evil was nothing more than a denial of God and his creation. To use a knife to stab someone is to misuse something good, but it does not make the knife itself an evil thing. Similarly, to use the mind for purposes other than those which God intended is to misuse the mind, but that does not mean the mind itself is evil.

By now, Augustine, at age thirty-two, was ready for conversion. It happened suddenly, and like so many great spiritual events, in a garden. Augustine was strolling among the flowers in Milan, when he heard a child singing, "Take up and read, take up and read." Perplexed, he took the first book he came across — the Epistles of Paul — opened it to a random page, and began to read. It said,

"Let us conduct ourselves becomingly as is the day, not in reveling and in drunkenness, not in debauchery and licentiousness, not in quarreling and jealousy. But put on the Lord Jesus, and make no provision for the flesh, to gratify its desires" (Romans 13:13-14).

Augustine shut the book. He felt quite calm, he writes. Everything just fell into place. There was nothing intellectual about his conversion; it was really so simple, like a child's nursery rhyme. As the modern phrase goes, Augustine was born again. Later he would work on his intellectual synthesis of Platonic and Christian thought. For now, he just went home and told his mother that he wanted to be baptized; she was ecstatic. Bishop Ambrose, who later would be canonized, performed the ceremony.

After his conversion Augustine found the key to understanding God: "Believe and you will understand." Until then he wanted his intellect to grasp God's truth before he would embrace it with his heart. Now he saw that faith is the first step, and rational evidence the second. And because faith was preeminent, Augustine focused his later writings on the dynamic between the soul and God, the truths taught by revelation. Augustine never seemed preoccupied with "proving" God's existence and his attributes, along with the rest of Christian doctrine. "A man who has faith in you, O Lord, owns all the world," he wrote in the *Confessions*. "Such a man, though he may not know the track of the Great Bear, is better by far than another who measures the sky and counts the stars and weighs the elements, but neglects you who allot to all things their size, number, and weight."

Unfortunately, his mother, Monica, died a few months after her son's conversion in 387; Augustine and

Adeodatus attended the funeral, and both wept. After burying his mother, Augustine returned to north Africa with the intent of becoming a monk. He was filled with God's light and holiness. "How do I love God?" he asks. "It's as though my soul is bathed in light that is not bound by space; when it listens to sound that never dies away; when it breathes fragrance that is not borne on the wind; when it tastes food that is never consumed by the eating; when it clings to an embrace from which it is not severed by the fulfillment of desire."

It is sometimes thought that a conversion to Christianity means a surrender of the intellect to God, which means a suspension of the critical intellect. The last books of Augustine's *Confessions* refute this popular prejudice. They show, on the contrary, that God's light brightens the human understanding. Augustine discusses the profound question of the creation of the universe toward the end of his great book.

There are several intriguing and provoking thoughts in this section. Of what did God make heaven and earth, Augustine asks. And where? "Clearly it was not in heaven or on earth that you made them," Augustine tells God. "Nor did you have in your hand any matter from which you could make heaven and earth, for where could you have obtained matter which you had not yet created?" It was in God's word, Augustine concludes, that heaven and earth were made.

"But how did you speak?" Augustine probes further. After all, speech is expressed through the motion of a created thing. Augustine realizes that God's "word is silent and eternal. It is different from the words which sound in time." Indeed God's word is an expression of God's will; it is not speech at all. "In your word all is uttered at one and the same time, yet eternally."

Yet God has made his word audible and visible to temporal beings, us. Thus we have the Bible. Augustine is impatient with biblical scholars of his day, the forerunners of many we see around us in our time, who discount Scripture as a metaphorical text to be understood as the imperfect work of fishermen and farmers. While Moses and the apostles may indeed have been simple folk, their writings reflect God's inspiration and therefore are without error. Augustine concedes that texts may have multiple interpretations, all true. But when men deny the truth of Scripture, Augustine remarks, it is hard for him to control his impatience. "They speak as they do," he writes, "not because they are men of God or because they have seen in the heart of Moses, but simply because they are proud. They are in love with their own opinions."

When the Bible says God created heaven and earth, Augustine says, that is exactly what it means. Augustine's humorous answer to those who ask, "What was God doing before he made heaven and earth?" is "He was preparing hell for people who pry into mysteries." His serious answer is that, no, God didn't spend eons in idleness, because "how could those countless ages have elapsed when you, the Creator, had not yet created them?" Time itself was created by God when he made heaven and earth.

Augustine follows this with a discussion of the nature of time that is of great philosophical depth. "I read the Scriptures carefully to discover whether it was seven or eight times that you saw that your works were good, when they pleased you," he tells God. "But realizing that your vision is outside time, I wondered about this. . . . Why do you tell me that your vision is not subject to time, and yet here your Scripture tells me that day by day you looked at what you had made and saw that it was good?" Augustine prayed about this and God answered him: "What my Scriptures say, I say. But the Scriptures speak in time, whereas time does not affect my word, which stands for ever, equal with me in eternity. While you see those things in time, it is not in time that I see them." Augustine is pleased and satisfied with this reply.

Ultimately the truths of God must be found by the heart that seeks God, Augustine ends. Addressing God, he asks, "What man can teach another to understand this truth? What angel can teach it to an angel? What angel can teach it to a man? We must ask it of you, seek it in you; we must knock at your door. Only then shall we receive what we ask and find what we seek, only then will the door be opened unto us."

His aspiration to be an anchorite was never fulfilled; fully conscious of his talents, the Church made him bishop of Hippo. But rather than settle down to administrative detail, Augustine launched into an intellectual crusade against Christian heresies — Donatism, Pelagianism, and even Manicheanism. It is in large part due to his ferocious resistance that these once-rampant heresies are now historical footnotes.

In the year 400 Augustine started work on one of his greatest theological treatises, *De Trinitate* (literally, "Concerning the Trinity"), which would comprise fifteen books. After the *Confessions*, perhaps his most famous work is *De Civitate Dei* ("Concerning the City of God"), a majestic account of the Christian view of civilization, written against the lurid background of the barbarian invasions of western Europe and northern Africa. Altogether Augustine's output was prolific; surviving are 113 books and treatises, over 200 letters, and more than 500 sermons.

In the year 430 the Vandals invaded north Africa and laid siege to the town of Hippo. In the fourth month of the siege, on August 28, 430, Augustine died. The barbarians eventually razed the city, though the cathedral with Augustine's body and his library were left intact. In 497 Augustine's remains were taken to Sardinia, where they remained until the eighth century. But the Saracens repeatedly raided the island; so to save Augustine's body from desecration, the king ordered it transported to Pavia in northern Italy, where it was reinterred. Augustine's soul was by now, of course, in another place.

The irony of Augustine's life is that, up to his death, he remained what Aristotle called a "eudaemonist," that is, he regarded happiness acquired through wisdom as the *raison d'être* for both philosophy and religion. Only he believed that this happiness comes from God and God alone. The skeptic searches for happiness through his philosophy, but his philosophy can never give him the thing for which he thirsts, namely truth; so he is perennially discontented. But the Christian loves someone who is permanent and independent, so happiness is eternal. All other pleasures are fleeting.

boethius's

consolation of philosophy

BOETHIUS'S *Consolation of Philosophy* is regarded as "the most popular Christian work of the Middle Ages," yet curiously it contains no Catholic theology, no quotations from the Bible, and no references to Jesus Christ. In fact, the sources most heavily drawn upon are Plato, Aristotle, and other classical philosophers. But the value of the *Consolation* — the reason it was such a delight and inspiration to such Catholic thinkers and artists as Thomas Aquinas and Dante — is its superb application of Greek concepts to Christian problems. The *Consolation* provides profound answers to two of the questions that have most plagued Catholic theologians: if God is truly all-compassionate and all-just, then why is there suffering in the world, and why do good men suffer while evil is rewarded? Second, if God is truly omniscient, if he has foreknowledge of what is going to happen in the world, then doesn't that mean it is already decided and known whether each of us will be good or evil, in which case how can it be maintained that we have a free will?

The *Consolation* is the "book of the most serene and kindly wisdom that the Middle Ages knew," according to critic W.P. Ker. "It restores a Platonic tradition, or even something older and simpler in Greek philosophy, at a time when simplicity and clearness of thought were about to be overwhelmed." Ker's point is that the Middle Ages were a time of theological complexity — dogmas were refined, elaborate heresies were defined, paradigms were constructed with the greatest care. To the twentieth-century reader much of this minute analysis seems a bit dull and beside the point. Perhaps this reflects more on the modern-day reader than on the texts themselves. But Boethius can be read with pleasure by anyone willing to apply a little concentration. His prose avoids the density and complexity of later medieval work. Ker goes so far as to say that the lucidity of the *Consolation* "saved the thought of the Middle Ages."

Although the *Consolation* is primarily a philosophical tract, it is best appreciated by understanding the circumstances under which it was written, for they were dire. Boethius wrote this book while he was sitting desolately in an Italian jail, waiting to be executed. In part, the *Consolation* was an effort by its author to persuade posterity that he was losing his head unjustly; in this Boethius is unsuccessful — the reader is not given enough information to feel competent to pass judgment on his case. But in his main project Boethius grandly succeeds: he gives us a new way to think about fate, about suffering and reward, about God's providence, about predestination and our ability to choose between right and wrong.

Although the *Consolation* is Boethius's most important work, he is also known for much else. More than anyone else, he transmitted Greek philosophy to the Christian world. He is known as "the last Roman philosopher, the first medieval scholastic." He wrote a brilliant commentary to Porphyry's *Introduction to the Categories of Aristotle*, in addition to writing and analyzing several original texts of Aristotle. He knew Plato better than any man of his time. He translated Cicero's *Topics*. His treatise on music remained a required text at Oxford until the eighteenth century. Moreover, he wrote five independent works of his own on logic, which are distinguished for their astute definitions of philosophical terms, definitions which became standard fare in the lexicon of the medieval theologian.

The *Consolation of Philosophy*, Boethius's magnum opus, had a far-reaching impact. It is safe to say that wherever there were good books in the Middle Ages, a copy of the *Consolation* could be found. The strength of the work is that it combines the best features of the greatest of Greek philosophers: the poetic imagination of Plato and the ordered rationalism of Aristotle. And the *Consolation* was popular even after the medieval period when other books such as Augustine's *Confessions* were put aside. King Alfred treasured Boethius's work so much that he translated it himself, as did the poet Geoffrey Chaucer. Sir Thomas More (who was beheaded in 1535 and canonized four hundred years later, in 1935) had Boethius's *Consolation* in mind when he wrote his own reflections during imprisonment. Queen Elizabeth (1533-1603) attempted her own translation. And even the historian Gibbon, so otherwise reticent in his praise, called the *Consolation* "a book not unworthy of Plato or Tully." For hundreds of years Boethius was read and memorized by Catholic theologians and clergy, who drew on his immense knowledge of philosophy and his brilliant synthesis of classical and Christian civilization.

The reason Boethius's knowledge of antiquity was so valuable was that by the late fifth century, scholars of Greek philosophy were rare; that culture had been virtually wiped out by hordes of barbarians from northern

Europe. These Vandals, Goths, Huns, and Lombards stormed south and simply razed monuments. What they could not loot they burned. Once they got complete surrender from the local people, they stopped destroying and tried to piece together the vanquished culture so that they could rule the people. But the damage was done. For example, Aristotle, along with Plato the preeminent thinker of antiquity, was only known in fragments to the early Middle Ages; most of his writings would not be discovered until a thousand years after Christ. That is why the common reference to this historical period as the "Dark Ages" is somewhat justified.

Boethius's classical knowledge is, in large part, due to his background. He was born Anicius Manlius Severinus Boethius around 480, the scion of the great Anician family of Rome. Among his ancestors were many consuls, two emperors, and a pope. But his family lived in turbulent times. Rome had been invaded and sacked by the barbarians. Italy was being ruled by the barbarian king Odoacer.* Boethius's father agreed to serve as prefect of the city and administer the law for Odoacer, but this was a reluctant decision, because Romans were

---

*AUTHOR'S NOTE: Odoacer is also spelled Odovacar. The reader may notice what may appear to be misspellings of proper names throughout this book; they are simply variant spellings. Other examples include Ecgbert (for Egbert) and Aethelbert (for Ethelbert) in Chapter 3. In addition, dates and places may differ from those found in other works; the reader is advised that such seeming inconsistencies are common because historians do not completely agree on such details. The important thing to remember is that the purpose of this book is to acquaint the reader with the philosophies, thoughts, and insights of the personalities whose writings are the subject of this work.

loath to serve under the barbarians. Boethius's father, however, died suddenly around 489; that same year Odoacer was deposed by Theodoric of the Ostrogoths; in 493 Theodoric killed Odoacer, seventeen years after the date known in history as that of the fall of the Roman Empire: A.D. 476.

Boethius was raised by another great Roman family, that of Quintus Aurelius Memmius Symmachus, an outstanding Catholic and the most eloquent orator in the Roman senate which served the new ruler Theodoric. It was Symmachus who first introduced Boethius to classical literature and philosophy; later Boethius would marry Symmachus's daughter Rusticiana, who is affectionately described in the *Consolation*.

Boethius was quiet and studious by disposition. During his youth he read voraciously until he was thoroughly familiar with the whole range of Greek speculative thought. His knowledge was both deep and far-ranging; it included music, mathematics, astronomy, and physiology. His talents soon came to the attention of Theodoric, who even though a barbarian was a charismatic fellow and wanted capable people in his cabinet. Theodoric had already enticed other eminent Romans such as Ennodius and Cassiodorus into public service; now he courted the young genius Boethius.

At first Boethius was unwilling, but finally persuaded himself to serve his ruler by invoking a central argument in Plato's *Republic*. The Greek philosopher says cities would be best managed under the care of public-spirited philosophers; in the *Consolation* we read that Boethius conceived of himself as exactly this selfless administrator when he accepted the post of consul from Theodoric. Apparently he served with distinction; not only was he rapidly promoted to chief minister, but in 522 Theodoric honored him by appointing both Boethius's young sons joint consuls.

How, then, did Boethius plummet so far, from virtual head of state to prisoner awaiting the executioner? In the *Consolation* we learn that he was not politically astute. "In the struggle to defend justice I was always indifferent to the hatred inspired in men who wielded greater power than mine," Boethius writes. Indeed he launched intrepid attacks against two of Theodoric's ministers and fellow Goths, Cunigast and Trigguilla. On another occasion he protected the former consul Paulinus who, he tells us, the "palace dogs" were itching to devour. Clearly, Boethius made plenty of enemies, and it does not seem that he lost any sleep over them.

But finally they had their revenge. The actual circumstances are a bit fuzzy, both in the *Consolation* and other historical documents of the time. It seems that the barbarian ruler Theodoric was worried that the Roman senate did not feel a true loyalty to him and in fact were plotting to depose him. In the year 519 the rift between the Eastern and Western Catholic churches (called the Acacian schism) was healed; the bishops of the eastern center of Constantinople succumbed completely to Roman authority. But this strengthened Rome's hand at a time when Theodoric was paranoid that Romans in his cabinet were disloyal to him. Would they take an occasion such as this to revolt?

At this tense point Theodoric's men intercepted some conspiratorial letters apparently headed for Emperor Justin, then in Constantinople. The former consul Albinus was implicated. Boethius, believing him innocent, rushed to his defense, thinking that his outstanding record of public service would preserve his credibility. "False is the charge of the accuser," Boethius said. "But if Albinus did it, I and all the Senate too did it with one accord." This was not prudent rhetoric, because it played into Theodoric's deepest fears. Boethius's enemies, seeing their chance, leaped at his throat, implicating him in the treason controversy. To Boethius's frustration, Theodoric did not come to his aid; indeed he turned on the man he had once showered with laurels. Boethius was quickly convicted and sentenced to death.

Alone in prison, Boethius begins the *Consolation* (consisting of five books) with what he calls "a long, noisy display of grief." He is innocent, he swears; the evidence against him is forged. He inveighs against his accuser, Cyprian, and grows indignant at Theodoric. He is trying to find distractions and solace in the composition of verses expressing his grief, but this only exacerbates the pain. Self-pity can be cathartic for some, but not for Boethius. In the peak of his lamentations (Book I) the Muse of Philosophy appears to him, questions him regarding his grief, and promises him an ointment for his affliction. Boethius is skeptical but interested.

The book is a fusion of several literary genres. In part it is a monologue, in other respects a dialogue very much like that of Plato's *Republic*. Unlike the Platonic conversations, however, Boethius does not use various characters who converse with each other, but rather, his is a "sacred dialogue" between two parties, himself and his Muse, where there is no real argument between the two parties but in which he asks the questions and the Muse provides the convincing answers. This, then, is apocalyptic dialogue in which Boethius communes with a divine spirit and transcribes the holy wisdom, extracted through his questions, in the chapters of the *Consolation*. The conversation actually alternates with poems which are intended to liven up the discourse, and give the reader some respite from the pace of the argument. Sometimes, like the chorus of a Greek tragedy, the poems advance the narrative. On a few occasions they are merely meant as a sort of moral medication for Boethius's tortured soul. Generally the verse is of a high order, as for example this famous stanza, inspired by Plato's *Timaeus*:

Oh, grant, Almighty Father,
Grant us on reason's wing to soar aloft
To heaven's exalted height; grant us to see
The fount of good; grant us, the true light found,
To fix our steadfast eyes in vision clear
On you. Disperse the heavy mists of earth
And shine in your own splendor. For you are
The true serenity and perfect rest
Of every pious soul — to see your face,
The end and the beginning — one the guide,
The traveler, the pathway, and the goal.

The Muse of Philosophy, in Book II, begins by pointing out that Boethius is wrong to lament his fortune, because "fortune has not changed toward you. Change is her normal behavior, her true nature. In the very act of changing she has preserved her own particular constancy toward you. She was exactly the same when she was flattering you and luring you on with enticements of a false kind of happiness."

This soothes Boethius somewhat, but not much; he argues that even if fortune is always fickle, that does not change the fact that "there is no greater pain than to recall a happy time in wretchedness." And Boethius is thinking of his dear friend Symmachus, and of his wife and children. His Muse reminds him that he should be relieved they are safe, but his memories only intensify his longing to be reunited with them.

The Muse of Philosophy goes on to develop the paradox that "bad fortune is of more use to a man than good fortune. Good fortune seems to bring happiness, but deceives you with her smiles, whereas bad fortune is always truthful because by changing she shows her true fickleness."

According to the Muse, the happy man either realizes that fortune is fickle, in which case he isn't too happy about that fact; or he doesn't realize fortune's capriciousness, in which case "what kind of happiness can there be in ignorance?" But the unfortunate man has no illusions about fortune; thus knowing the truth about her he is happy.

This may seem a bit convoluted and implausible, but in fact Boethius is using a very old argument, Aristotle's in the *Ethics*, that "happiness is the activity of the soul in accordance with virtue." The idea is that the deepest desire of the soul is for truth; material possessions only satisfy desire temporarily, and in many cases they bring frustration. True happiness — as Boethius tells us in Book III — comes from the *summum bonum*: the supreme good or truth which all men consciously or unconsciously seek.

Boethius denies that bodily pleasures can bring true happiness to a human being. "If bodily pleasures can produce happiness," he writes, "there is no need to question whether animals are happy, since their whole aim in life is directed toward the fulfillment of their bodily needs." Certainly, he suggests, sensory fulfillment does not achieve a very high level of happiness. Man is different from the animal and there are certain intellectual and psychological pleasures that he experiences that are higher than those of the animal. The emotional relations between parents and children, for example, are of a much more complex nature than between animals and their young, who operate wholly on instinct.

Yet, says Boethius, "these roads to happiness are side-tracks and cannot bring us to the destination they promise. The evils with which they are beset are great. If you try to hoard money, you will have to grab it from others. If you want to be resplendent in the dignities of high office, you will have to grovel before the man who bestows it: in your desire to outdo others in high honor you will have to cheapen and humiliate yourself by begging. If you want power, you will have to expose yourself to the plots of your subjects and run dangerous risks. If fame is what you seek, you will find yourself on a hard road, drawn this way and that until you are worn with care." Besides, all these things are ephemeral.

"Goodness is the chief point upon which the pursuit of everything hinges and by which it is motivated," Boethius insists. "If a man wants to go riding for the sake of health, for example, it is not so much the motion of horse-riding he desires, so much as the resultant good health. Since, therefore, all things are desired for the sake of the good in them, no one desires them as much as the good itself." What is that good?

First the Muse of Philosophy proves that such a good must exist. Men recognize certain things as pretty good; this implies that they have some idea or standard of goodness; this goodness must exist if it is to be apprehended; this perfect goodness we call God. Boethius is not about to dispute God's existence; as he points out in Book IV, he is more interested in the question of how evil can be the fate of good men when a supposedly just God is in charge. This recalls Job's question in the Bible, "Why do the wicked live, reach old age, and grow mighty in power [while the good suffer]?" (21:7).

Here the Muse makes an ingenious argument: many wicked people are punished for their deeds, and those who are not are worse off than those who are. The reason? Punishment for an evil person is just. When an evil person is punished, his evil is diminished because it is mixed with the good of justice. "But when an evil man goes unpunished he acquires some extra evil in going scot-free, which is bad because of its injustice."

The good man, by contrast, should not worry about suffering evil or pain, because if he is truly good it cannot corrupt him. "A wise man ought no more to take ill when he clashes with fortune than a brave man ought to be upset by the sound of battle," the Muse says. After all, "for both of them their very distress is an opportunity, for the one to gain glory, and the other to strengthen his wisdom. That is why virtue gets its name, because it is firm in strength and unconquered by adversity." So the Muse seems to be saying that, for good and evil people alike, suffering should not be viewed as a sign of divine injustice; in fact it is a divine gift, because it is good for the soul. It inspires heroism in the good, and to the evil it gives a chance for atonement.

Unfortunately in his attempt to downplay the effects of evil, Boethius goes overboard. Using Plato's concepts, he argues that existence is good, evil is the absence of good, so evil is lack of existence. This nicely answers the question of whether God is capable of doing evil. After all, if God can do all things, the only thing God cannot do is nothing, and since evil is nothing, God cannot do evil. Boethius wrings this fabric of argument too tightly, though; he goes on to argue that because evil is nothing, evil men are powerless. For those of the twentieth century who have experienced atrocities perpetrated by such men as Hitler and Stalin, this statement fails to convince.

Mercifully, the Muse goes on to a discussion of chance. If chance is defined as an event without a cause, then there is no such thing as chance, the Muse says. Indeed the ancient philosophers were right about this: nothing can come out of nothing, *ex nihilo, nihil*. But there is a difference between chance and fate. When a result occurs which was other than the one intended, that's fate. If, say, a man digging in a field comes across a pot of gold, that's not *ex nihilo*, as the gold was actually buried there. But it was a coincidence of fate that this particular man, who happened to be digging there, found the gold.

Fate, however, is not quite the same thing as providence. According to the Muse, providence is divine reason itself; it is the planned order of things, and it is unchanging. Fate is the means by which providence achieves its objectives, and it *seems* to change wildly to the individuals it affects. But in fact fate is like a circle with providence at its center; nothing falls outside the orbit of the divine plan.

In these definitions of providence and fate, Boethius seems to have cleverly integrated two ideas: that of a swiftly revolving fate, and that of a guiding, motionless providence. Fate is the wheel which spins our plans every which way, and yet fate hinges on God, "the still point of the turning world," as the Muse terms him. This analogy also has implications for the human soul. The more it frees itself from material things and material desires, the nearer it comes to the spiritual source, the stability of the center, God's resting place.

The Muse's distinction between fate and providence deprives men of the right to criticize the evil in the world, because they blame this evil on fate, without realizing that fate is only a reflection of the orchestrated wisdom of providence, which they cannot see at work. Boethius gives the example of laymen who are surprised to see sweet things agree with some people's bodies and bitter things with others' bodies; but it is no surprise to the doctor who knows the difference between the two bodies, and between various kinds of sicknesses. "And the protector of the good and scourge of the wicked is none other than God, the mind's guide and physician." The argument really comes down to: trust God; he knows better.

Yet this line of argument raises a problem concerning the autonomy of the human will. After all, the claim that everything is subject to providence implies that nothing is subject to chance, or more precisely, *choice*. This raises the problem of free will which may fairly be called the greatest philosophic dilemma of all time. Boethius — in the fifth and final book of the *Consolation* — asks his Muse: How can a God who knows in advance what is going to happen disclaim responsibility for what does happen then? How can providence coexist with free will? "If God beholds all things and cannot be deceived, that must of necessity follow which his providence forsees to be to come. Hence, if from eternity he knows beforehand not only the deeds of men, but also their wills, there can be no free will." In other words, if men are driven to good or evil by the fixed necessity of what is to be, then all talk of vice and virtue is meaningless; everything is preordained.

It is not enough to answer, Boethius points out, that just because God knows something is going to happen, that does not mean he causes it to happen. It is not enough to reply that future events don't take place because God knows them, but rather the opposite: God knows them because they take place. This is a bad answer because it implies that temporal or worldly events — the actions of human beings — are the cause of the eternal foreknowledge of God. As Boethius puts it, "How absurd it is to say that the occurrence of temporal events governs and causes eternal prescience."

The skeptic is on strong ground when he raises the question of whether there can be any foreknowledge of things whose occurrence is not inevitable. But the Muse of Philosophy finds even stronger, and higher, ground to rebut him. She does this by giving a novel definition to the word "eternity," a definition that would alter future Christian understanding of the term. Eternity is not the same as perpetuity, the Muse says. Eternity is not just time stretched infinitely back into the past, and forward into the future. Rather, "Eternity is the whole and perfect possession of unlimited life at once."

Take a moment to ponder this. The Muse is really saying that eternity is outside time. To the extent that eternity concerns time, it is more about the quality of time than the quantity, about the concentration of time than its duration. When we say God is eternal we should not therefore think of him as within time, because this is what creates all the difficulties.

If we consider God outside time, then the problem of free will is solved. That is because what man perceives successively, as happening in time, God perceives simultaneously. There is no question of divine *foreknowledge* of anything. As the Muse puts it, "God abides for ever in the eternal Now." And even here, in using the word "now" the Muse does not mean a particular point in time, but a state of existence which is not dependent on time. This is all a bit hard to understand, the Muse concedes, for we all live in time and pass from the present to the future, and we are not familiar with anything set in

41

time which can "embrace simultaneously the whole extent of its life."

In giving this definition of eternity, Boethius is departing from his classical ancestors. Both Plato and Aristotle thought of eternity as perpetuity, as forever. They had no concept of the eternal present. In a number of early Christian thinkers, from Augustine to Boethius to Aquinas, we see a clever use of ancient philosophy up to the point where it is useful to break away, or build upon it new Catholic ideas of a personal God, a loving God — ideas completely alien to Plato and Aristotle, who could think only of God as a first cause, or a prime mover.

Once Boethius has accepted the Muse's definition of eternity, the Muse gets Boethius to assent to the proposition that "the knowledge of present things imposes no necessity on what is happening." This is really pretty obvious. All the Muse is saying is that if a man sees the sun rise, or another man walk, simply seeing this does not impose any condition on the action. In other words, for a man to merely observe this is not for him to, in any way, diminish the freedom of the sun to rise and of the man to walk.

So, similarly, the Muse says, for God to simply perceive present actions by men is not to eliminate human freedom. For God to watch men commit acts of sin or practice virtue before his eyes is not for him to affect those acts. He is like a man in a tall tower, watching the activity on the street, or a spectator at a sporting event. Of course, God can affect the activity, but he chooses not to, because he wants man to use the freedom he has been given. "Present events," the Muse says, "when considered with reference to God's sight of them, do happen necessarily as a result of the condition of divine knowledge; but when considered in themselves they do not lose the absolute freedom of their nature."

But if God's perception of present actions does not affect human freedom, and since God perceives all events — past, present, and future — simultaneously, in a simultaneous present, that means that God imposes no restrictions on free will. There is freedom, there is providence, but neither compromises the other.

This notion of eternity, it should be noted, has implications for us today. We think too much of "progress" as something that is time-bound; we are always bemoaning attempts to "turn back the clock"; we think the future is worthwhile for its own sake. We often do not have goals which lie outside time, goals which concern not what we are going to *do* tomorrow but what we *are*. We are dimmed to that medieval sense of the goal that makes life supremely worth living for its own sake. Boethius can help us refocus attention on these weaknesses.

With her explanation of the compatibility of providence and human freedom, the Muse rests her case, and Boethius is ready for death. Like Socrates, he is indifferent to its final outcome. Yet, the title of Boethius's book should not mislead its reader as to the reason for Boethius's readiness to accept death. Boethius did not find the answer to his woes in the act of philosophizing per se. Philosophy in itself was not enough; it had to be the right philosophy. Only in discovering satisfactory answers to the dilemmas of the soul, in vindicating divine justice, in upholding the moral order of the universe, in reaffirming human freedom, only then did Boethius at last find his consolation.

This is just as well, because Boethius met a very bad end. He knew he was going to die, but not how brutal it would turn out to be. Apparently his executioners botched the job. They are said to have pulled the rope so tightly around his neck that his eyes popped out. And even when they had strung him up he took so long to die that they had to finally club him to death. It also turns out that the Muse's assurances about the health of Symmachus were premature, because in 525, the year after Boethius's death, Symmachus was arrested, taken to Ravenna, and executed. The reason was that Theodoric feared that Symmachus might plot to kill him to avenge Boethius's death.

Boethius was buried in the Cathedral Church of Ticenum. In the eighth century the body is believed to have been moved to the church of San Pietro in Ciel d'Oro. At any rate, the poet Dante thought so, because in his immortal *Divine Comedy* we find Boethius in the highest circle of heaven. Dante calls him "the sainted soul, who unmasked the deceitful world . . . living in martyrdom in Cieldauro."

Was Boethius a martyr? The entire Middle Ages thought so. After all, his ruler Theodoric was a believer in the Arian heresy, which denied the Catholic doctrine of the Trinity. And yet there is no evidence that Boethius suffered religious persecution. Certainly religious and political factors were intertwined in the scandal which led to his downfall. But for all his brute qualities Theodoric is known to have been a defender of religious freedom: Catholics, Arians, and even Jews were protected in the exercise of their faith. Boethius himself admits this.

Boethius's death was political. His life was devoted to philosophy. His greatest work, the *Consolation*, abounds with references to Euripides, Aristotle, Homer, Claudian, Catullus, Plato, Ovid, and Seneca, but none to Christ. So we are back to our old question: Why does

Boethius, writing in the last days before his death, write about philosophy and not theology, about Plato but not Jesus, about freedom but not the Resurrection? Why is philosophy his *summum vitae solamen* — his main solace in life — and not the Bible?

We can never know for sure, but some answers may be suggested. We know Boethius was a Catholic and a believer. He wrote five tractates, or discourses, on theology and they are all completely orthodox. It has been suggested that he repudiated Christianity in the last days before his death, but a writer as honest as Boethius would have said so, if this had actually been the case.

More likely Boethius held the view, in contrast with that of Augustine, that philosophy and theology belong to somewhat separate spheres, that they perform different functions, and yet that it is possible to arrive at an understanding of God's greatness and justice through either. Boethius does not have Augustine's suspicious view of reason: he sees that Plato and Aristotle, who predated Christ and had no access to Christian doctrine, nevertheless arrived at ideas of God as creator and dispenser of justice which astonishingly paralleled Christian ones. Perhaps Boethius wanted to show that it was possible to scale the heights of Christian truth through philosophy — and behind his arguments, unseen but known to God, shines forth that irrational, childlike faith in the personal love and grace of Christ.

bede's

ecclesiastical history

THE Venerable Bede is not well known outside of ecclesiastical circles today. Yet during the eighth century he was the best-known scholar and historian in Europe. He produced nothing as original as Augustine's *Confessions* or Aquinas's *Summa*. But his *Ecclesiastical History of the English Nation* is undoubtedly the most systematic account we have of how Christianity spread throughout most of Europe. Saint Bede's main strength was his range and synthetic ability — he brought together diverse dates and details into a convincing historical narrative. Without him modern historians would have, in their retrospective of the last two thousand years of civilization, a large chasm.

Why the need for such a history? Because spreading a religion can be no less difficult than founding one. Christ never traveled more than a radius of a few hundred miles during his lifetime, and though his apostles preached ardently and inspiredly after his death, they could scarcely reach the surrounding area and Europe, let alone the world. Christianity did spread quickly through the Mediterranean, triumphing even over sophisticated philosophies of antiquity. These philosophies had served Rome well in its greatness, but they were not helping much in its decadence — indeed they were suspected of furthering the degeneracy of its citizens — and the people of Italy were much attracted to the simplicity of the Catholic faith: its appeal to a personal God and its promise of eternal life.

But with the barbarian invasions in Italy and southern Europe, the whole climate changed. Into the walls of the ancient cities poured Germanic tribes adept at little other than plunder, and down came the great monuments and churches and Roman arenas. The invaders were pagans who worshiped strange gods, and who resolved to wipe out both Platonism and Christianity. Fortunately civilization has a way of triumphing over barbarism, even when the barbarians have the weapons. Instead of the Huns and the Lombards converting the Christians, the opposite occurred — but not immediately, and often with great struggle on the part of the Christians. This process of Christianizing barbarian Europe is chronicled in Bede's *Ecclesiastical History*. It, more than any other document, explains how Europe went from a rude, idol-worshiping continent to an almost universally Christian nation. The development of Catholic Church tradition is intimately connected with these developments.

Bede's historical accomplishment becomes truly staggering when you consider his environs. He was born around 673 of lowly parents in Northumbria, England, where at the age of seven he was placed in the monastery at Wearmouth. Between this and a neighboring monastery, Jarrow, Bede would spend the rest of his life. So he was not exactly a cosmopolitan personality. Nor did he live a particularly exciting life — no lapses into dangerous heresy, no unchaste women to draw him into sin; in fact, probably Bede's most exciting childhood experience was getting over a speech impediment, which he did by composing verses and reciting them aloud.

Bede's boyhood is preserved in the anonymous *Life of Abbot Ceolfrid*, where we read about the horrible plague of 686 which killed all the monks capable of performing church services in the monastery "with the exception of the abbot himself and one boy reared and educated by him." At first Ceolfrid suspended the singing of psalms and antiphons until he could recruit new choirboys and helpers, but this filled him with such regret that the young Bede offered to learn and perform the various duties of a choirmonk so that services could proceed in full ritual. It is a tribute to Bede's versatility and intelligence that he was able to master so varied a slate of duties. Also we see how he developed the discipline to perform church rituals daily from a very early age.

Monastery life was extremely pious and routinized. It was conducted according to the famous Rule of Saint Benedict. This rule, developed around the sixth century, set forth the way a Christian monk should live. Spartan diets, regular incantations and prayers, the breaking of the bread in the sacrament of the Holy Eucharist, self-mortification, charity toward others — all these were highly recommended. But Benedict cautioned against the more imaginative forms of self-torture that early Christian monks were attempting, to prove their devotion to Christ.

This sort of exhibitionism had its roots in pride, Benedict saw, and God did not give us bodies to tear them apart. The main feature of the Benedictine rule was that it was sensible asceticism — it kept monks at the standard of living of a healthy peasant, plus it ensured orthodox Catholic beliefs and the practice of the faith. England was dotted with monasteries following this format during Bede's time. Bede's life was therefore, in many respects, very normal.

It should not be supposed that these monasteries were, as skeptics would later charge, dens of ignorance and iniquity. There was some corruption, human nature being what it is; but it was the exception, not the standard — and Bede inveighed against it in a famous letter to Ecgbert, archbishop of York. As for learning, the monasteries were the universities of their day — they were veritable founts of knowledge, and they stored, developed, and disseminated information all across Europe. To be in a monastery may have been physically stifling, but intellectually it was liberating, and Bede got the finest education available at the time.

He knew Greek, Latin, and, more than likely, some Hebrew. He based many of his theological works on the writings of the early Church Fathers. He knew some of Plato's works, Ptolemaic astronomy, and the Bible virtually by heart. Yet his wide intellectual interests never detracted from his monastic commitment. He did all the chores that the other monks did — washing the floor; sowing seeds; threshing; feeding and milking cattle; carpentering; cooking. And he never missed his hours of prayer, even though as his fame as a historian spread his bishop exempted him from some spiritual duties. "Angels visit our hours of prayer," Bede wrote. "What if they did not find me there? Would they not say: Where is Bede? Why does he not come with the brethren to the appointed hours of prayer?"

This orthodoxy is reflected in the *Ecclesiastical History*. It makes an important difference, because whenever you are dealing with the "inculturation" of Catholicism — the implantation of the faith in a pagan culture — the question arises: What compromise is the culture going to make to accommodate Christianity, and vice versa? Catholicism preserved its purity through the Middle Ages by not admitting the vice versa: it would allow different cultures to worship in different ways, but it would insist that they worship the same thing — the God who became man — and that they accept the immutable doctrines of the Catholic faith.

Bede approvingly gives the example of a letter sent by Pope Gregory the Great (who would eventually be proclaimed a saint) to one Abbot Mellitus who was converting pagans in England. The abbot inquired how the pagan temples were to be treated. They were not to be razed, Gregory wrote, but only the pagan idols they housed. If the temples were well built, they were to be blessed and used for Holy Mass so that the converts could continue to pray in familiar places. Nor should the pagans be deprived of making their customary sacrifices of oxen and goats — only these should be killed according to the Old Testament fashion, and offered up to the Christian God. It is wise to remember these principles when we hear modern Catholic theologians call upon the Church to abandon sacred doctrines to appease the customs of certain African tribes, such as polygamy. Yet Bede's *History* shows that attempts to baptize pagan culture were not always altogether successful. For example, Redwald, king of the East Saxons, had in the same temple an altar to Christ and another one dedicated to pagan deities. Similarly a Frankish casket of this period has, on one side, a heathen story of massacre, and on the other, a beautiful portrait of the Adoration of the Magi.

Because of his intelligence and devotion, Bede was made a deacon by his bishop, John of Beverly, at the age of nineteen, even though canon law stipulated that the minimum age was twenty-five. Exceptions could be made only for men of outstanding holiness — apparently Bede qualified. He studied for the priesthood in his abbot Benedict Biscop's well-stocked library; he was ordained in 703. His first books contained elementary instruction for pupils in the monastery. Later, he would compose almost sixty books, including a treatise on music, several hagiographical works, and profound commentaries on the Scriptures and on the works of the four great Latin Fathers — Augustine, Jerome, Ambrose, and Gregory.

His greatest work, however, he saved for the end. For the *Ecclesiastical History* he drew on his enormous reservoir of knowledge, plus numerous reputable authorities. His inspiration to write the *History* came from Albinus, abbot of a monastery founded by Augustine of Canterbury. His model for the *History* was the ecclesiastical history of Eusebius, as translated and continued by Rufinus. But Bede goes much further than Eusebius — having access to a wider range of materials, plus a more refined historical sense: he presents his facts meticulously, cites his sources, and has the eye for anecdote and detail which make history come alive. No wonder he is called the "Father of English History."

The *History* is divided into five books of about the same number of chapters and length. Bede's work spans almost eight hundred years, from the Roman invasion of Britain to within a few years of Bede's own death in 735. But although Bede begins his narrative as far back as Caesar's rule in Rome, the main part of the *History* is concerned with the period from A.D. 605 to 731. Since the seventh century is known as the Age of Conversion, Bede's material is of immense value to Catholics concerned with their origins and past. And the period between the late 600s and the beginning of the eighth century, Bede's own, was the Golden Age of British Catholicism. So we see the flickering flames of Catholicism turn into a virtual conflagration in Europe, as the continent is brought into the faith, and then we see the fires settle down into a bright and constant blaze — the order and self-purification of monastic Christian life.

Long before Bede's time Pope Gregory the Great, writing to Eulogius, bishop of Alexandria, described the English as a people who lived in an irrelevant corner of the world and placed their trust in sticks and stones. In 596 Gregory sent the missionary Augustine (not the Augustine of the *Confessions*) with monks from Rome to Britain to preach the Catholic faith. Augustine landed at Thanet, where he was greeted by Aethelbert, king of Kent. Aethelbert's wife was Christian, but the king himself was without religion. Augustine preached to him, but Aethelbert said he would not convert, though he would allow the Christians to live and preach in peace. In Canterbury the Christians set up a monastery at St. Martin and began to live according to the Benedictine rule. People came in great numbers and were baptized.

Christianity began to spread through conversion, through intermarriage between Christians and pagans, and through conquest by proselytizing kings. Bede's tone in describing this can only be described as providential — as all part of God's plan; if we do not read it this way, he may strike as cruel. For example, he tells of the Isle of Wight, one of the last bastions of English heathenism, and one that King Caedwella of Wessex was resolved to conquer and convert. The king swore that if he was successful, he would give one third of the land he took to the Catholic Church. His troops smashed into Wight, laying waste and burning everything in sight. Eventually he did prevail, and Bishop Wilfred of Sussex accepted the donation of land. Bede tells us about two brothers of the vanquished king who fled to Stoneham. King Caedwella found out, and sent troops to massacre them. The local abbot interceded for the boys, asking for a stay of execution so he could baptize them. They accepted Christ and "when the executioners came upon them, they gladly underwent the temporal death whereby they were assured that they would pass into eternal life." Bede tells us all this without a trace of horror, as though it was a perfectly normal happening — and in those days, it was.

England was dominated by the Celtic people who lived for centuries under the Roman Empire. But as Rome faltered and withdrew its curtain of protection, the Celts became vulnerable to invaders from northern Europe — Angles, Saxons, Jutes, and others. They were driven west into increasingly remote parts of Britain, and even here they were set upon by Irish pirates who operated on land and sea. In Devon, Wales, Cumberland, and Scotland the Celts tried to maintain their native customs and autonomy. Some practiced a Christian faith imported to Britain in the fourth century after Christ, when Rome converted under Emperor Constantine. The Picts and the Scots hated Britain as well as Rome, regarding both cultures as alien. Bede describes how these different and mutually hostile peoples were all converted to Catholicism. The Church, Bede believes, gave the various tribes a common banner of faith, a purpose of being that transcended their local customs, and it brought them into contact with the rest of Christendom so that they could overcome their semibarbaric ways and learn from the art, literature, and philosophy of Christian Rome.

Slowly, the Christian influence spread. Columba and Aidan brought the Gospel to the north; Ninian to the

Picts; Patrick to the Irish; David and others to the Celts of Cornwall; and Augustine to the newly established Saxons. Bede describes how the Celtic customs were gradually overcome and replaced by those of the Roman Church. The nomadic and spiritualist Celtic priest, who wielded no secular authority and had no administrative responsibility, gave way to the diocesan system, where priests were not only in charge of spiritual matters but also in charge of running the churches and monasteries. Certainly the early fervor of the Celtic missionaries contributed to the spread of the Church, Bede realizes, for who can better the fervor of one who does nothing but pray and proselytize? Yet as the Church grew and spread, Bede tells us, there was need for a better managed system than the Celts had develped, a system that would bring a measure of order and stability to the new churches.

Christianity first spread to Northumbria, Bede's area, around 625. King Edwin of Northumbria married Aethelberg, daughter of King Aethelbert and a Christian. Although Aethelbert remained a pagan to his death, his Catholic wife told Edwin that she would not permit him, a pagan, to sleep with her Christian daughter. Edwin promised he would convert if he found Christianity sensible, and if he was successful in defeating a rival king who tried to have him assassinated. Edwin did find merit to Catholicism, and he led a victorious expedition against the West Saxons, but still he was reluctant.

Then Bede gives us an exhortation to Edwin to convert by one of his Christian advisers, a passage which has become the most famous in the *Ecclesiastical History*: "This, O King, the present life of men on earth, in comparison with that time which is unknown to us, appears to me to be as if, when you are sitting at supper with your aldermen in the winter time, and a fire is lighted in the midst and the hall warmed, but everywhere outside the storms of wintry rain and snow are raging, a sparrow should come and fly rapidly through the hall, coming in at one door and out immediately through the other. While it is inside it is not touched by the storm of winter, but yet that tiny space of calm gone in a moment, from winter at once returning to winter, it is lost to your sight. Thus this life of men appears for a little while, but of what is to follow or what went before, we are entirely ignorant. Hence, if this new teaching brings greater certainty about the unknown, it seems fit to be followed."

Edwin did convert and he established, Bede tells us, such an orderly Christian state that if a woman with her newborn child walked through Northumbria at night she would feel completely safe.

The conversion of the South Saxons was mainly accomplished through the efforts of Bishop Wilfred of Northumbria, who returned to England from Rome in 680. As Wilfrid approached the island, hundreds of pagans, led by their chief priest, began to chant curses at the Christians. At this point one of Wilfred's monks took up a stone and, like David before Goliath, hurled it at the wizard's forehead, slaying him on the spot. This broke the will of the pagans, who immediately became subservient to the Roman visitors.

Although Catholicism was becoming rooted in Kent and Northumbria, much of the land now called Middlesex, Hertfordshire, and Surrey remained pagan. And other areas such as Essex were lapsing into paganism — it is one thing to convert barbarians, another to maintain their allegiance to orthodoxy and Catholic practice. Fortunately in 668 a little-known monk was appointed bishop of Canterbury; this Theodore of Tarsus would expand Catholicism into territories previously untouched. In the twenty-one years Theodore would hold the post of archbishop of Canterbury, he would probably do more for that see than anyone else in history.

Theodore arrived in England in May of 668, a few years before Bede's birth. Theodore's tenure comprised the years of Bede's youth, and later Bede would look back on them as the happiest times for English Catholicism. The faith was vital then — penetrating the remotest and fiercest hamlets, thanks to the dedication of Theodore's tireless monks. Theodore also established an effective diocesan organization which so many other bishops lacked. It was through this ecclesiastical order that missionary work could be executed in the most systematic way; also channels were established for dealing with (that is, stamping out) heresy.

Although Bede shows great sympathy for the various Germanic cultures, he is relentless in defending the imposition of orthodoxy on the converted peoples. Commenting on the Pelagian heresy which threatened to spread in England, Bede notes that "Pelagius, a Briton, spread far and near the infection of his perfidious doctrine against the assistance of divine grace, being seconded by Julianus of Campania, whose anger was kindled by the loss of his bishopric, of which he had been justly deprived. Saint Augustine and other orthodox Fathers quoted many thousand Catholic sources against them, yet they would not correct their madness; on the contrary, their folly was increased by contradiction, and they refused to embrace the truth." Bede harshly criticized British clergy who failed to observe Easter according to the date and rites of the Roman Catholic Church.

The *Ecclesiastical History* gives us a vivid account of life in the various monasteries around England.

Although all abided by some version of the Benedictine rule, there is a surprising variety of styles of worship and practice. Unfortunately during Bede's lifetime there was a slackening of ecclesiastical discipline in some areas; in one strange passage Bede describes a penitential (a manual on penances) by Bishop Theodore requiring bishops and priests who are "incorrigible drunkards" to step down. But for every failing cleric or monastery there were a hundred vital ones, and Bede gives at length an account of the monastery run by one Hilda. That a woman should head an entire monastic community may surprise us, but this Hilda was no ordinary nun — in fact, her community became famous throughout Britain for its austerity and piety. And Hilda, who was also something of an intellectual, had quite an influence persuading Catholic converts to accept the Roman (as opposed to the Scottish) date for Easter. This was a much sorer point than we can today imagine.

Bede's *History* continues into his present day. What is interesting is that because of his own voluminous writings he made the monasteries of Wearmouth and Jarrow famous in Europe. Thus it is appropriate that their story be included in Bede's story of Catholicism in England. In fact, Bede has created some of the history that he then set down to write.

Wearmouth and Jarrow were both founded by Benedict Biscop through land grants from Ecgfrith of Northumbria. As the number of monks at these monasteries grew, Biscop had to negotiate for more land for Jarrow. This was not donated by the king but sold. Apparently Ecgfrith gave Biscop several acres in return for — a single book. Books were rare in the Middle Ages, and before the age of printing they were very laborious to produce. Bede was first at Wearmouth and later transferred to

Jarrow. He learned much of what he did from Benedict, and of the great monk's death Bede gives us a moving account in the *Ecclesiastical History*. For several weeks the monks wept for their beloved brother. They refused to sleep, spending the nights singing in the chapel, reciting the Gospels, and giving the Viaticum. Benedict was succeeded by the abbot Coelfrith, whose biography Bede would later write.

In 685 King Ecgfrith was killed in a battle against the Picts. Bede was obliged to Ecgfrith, because he had endowed both Wearmouth and Jarrow, yet he wrote that the king's death was a punishment for sins he had committed in refusing to listen to those who had tried to dissuade him from sending an army against the Irish in 684 and the Picts in 685. Orthodox as he was, Bede resented attempts by Christian kings to conquer and convert by force — he described the Irishmen killed by Ecgfrith's armies as "unoffending people, always most friendly to the English nation."

Bede's *History* is no collage of names and dates. It is full of vivid character sketches. Bede tells us about the abbot Eosterwin who "remained so humble that he loved to tresh and winnow, milk cows and ewes, and occupy himself obediently in the bakery, garden, kitchen, and all the work of the monastery." Yet this same Eosterwin "corrected offenders with regular discipline" and wielded undisputed and total authority in the monastery. We see in Eosterwin what many perceive as true spiritual leadership: humility combined with authority, the need for leaders to set an example.

Bede's *Ecclesiastical History*, brilliant in scope though it is, does have flaws that are impossible to ignore. To Bede's credit he admits that a good deal of his information is secondhand. "But I did not think that error should be imputed to me when I follow the authority of the great Catholic Doctors. I thought I should adopt without scruple what I found in their works." Bede does get some facts wrong, such as the date of Saint Alban's martyrdom, but he is quick to spot internal contradictions in accounts he quotes — these he warns his readers about.

It is not surprising that we find, in Bede, that charming medieval habit of getting more out of numbers than there is in them. Few medieval thinkers — not even Aquinas and Dante — are free of this metaphysics of algebra. For example, Bede announces that it is significant that the number of workmen building Solomon's temple is 30,000. Three is the number of the Trinity. The Temple is said to have been built 480 years after the Exodus, which leads Bede to note that 480 equals 4 times 120. If you didn't know, 4 is the number of evangelical perfection, while 120 is the number of years Moses lived. Bede's naïveté did not extend to predicting dates for the end of the world; indeed he rejected this common medieval practice and affirmed, with Saint Augustine, that the time of Christ's Second Coming is concealed from human eyes.

And what are we to make of Bede's miracles? A handful we can accept, perhaps, but there seems to be a miracle on every page. In the first chapter of the *History* Bede tells us about pages of books brought by Christians from Ireland which "when put into water have cured persons bitten by serpents." Rivers dry up; incredible illnesses are healed; one executioner's eyes pop out at the moment that he chops off the martyr's head. And there are more mundane miracles — Saint Cuthbert stops at a hut for the night; his horse tugs at a straw from the roof, and down falls what turns out to be Cuthbert's evening meal: meat and bread wrapped in a piece of cloth. A bit later Cuthbert does penance before a wintry sea; in the morning two otters emerge from the ocean and warm his frozen feet with their breath.

It is tempting to be condescending toward Bede's credulity. But a few things should be kept in mind. Bede himself tells us that he is, in many cases, simply quoting Church Fathers whose credibility is unquestioned. Also, the saints who perform miracles are men of tremendous ascetical discipline — perhaps they developed mental powers of clairvoyance and healing. More likely, the devotion of their entire lives to God brought them special grace; Bede writes the cessation of miracles in latter times is largely due to man's sin. How often today do men and women sacrifice every pleasure in life — from good food to sex — for God's love? How many spend the hours praying the way the monks did? It is not surprising to Bede that those who love God more are given greater spiritual powers than those who love him less.

A fortnight before Easter in the year 735 Bede fell gravely ill, and had trouble breathing. He continued to give lessons to students at the monastery, even as his pain increased. He was losing his memory; once he began singing the antiphon for the *Magnificat*, "O rex gloriae," and burst into tears: then recovering himself, he had to start from the beginning. The day after the feast of the Ascension he was alone with one of his pupils, who was taking down notes he dictated. It was hard for Bede to go on, but despite the student's protestations, he insisted that he keep writing. As his energy began to leave his body, Bede summoned the priests, who said Mass for him and gave him the last sacraments. After this the boy, nervous and afraid, blurted out, "Sir, there is still a sentence which is not written down." Bede replied, "Well, then go ahead and write it." When the boy said, "It is finished," Bede sat back. "You have said the truth," he said. "It is finished." He sang the *Gloria Patri* and died.

Bede's death, said the great Alcuin, was like the extinction of a bright light. He was, during his lifetime, the most eminent scholar of the West. He helped England make its way from a brutish and barbarian nation to one of the bedrocks of the civilized Christian world. Many of Bede's pupils went on to notable achievements: his protégé Lullus, for example, was soon to become archbishop of Mainz. Bede's *Ecclesiastical History* is a classic not only because of its attention to detail and narrative power but also because Bede somehow synthesized the verve and passion of the Celtic race with the asceticism and discipline of the monks. Unfortunately his life was a brief epoch between periods of violence; soon after his death, the Danes would invade Northumbria and exterminate much of the culture that Bede had helped develop.

Only one question remains: Why is he called the Venerable Bede? A common speculation is that the title "venerable" generally preceded the given names of priests in Saint Bede's time. But there is another, more colorful explanation. A legend tells us that when Bede was a very old man and could not see well, some practical jokers, wishing to amuse themselves, told him that the church was full of people waiting for him to preach. Bede hurried to the pulpit and delivered a moving oration. At the end of it the angels, who alone filled the building, said, "Amen, thou venerable Bede." The story is apocryphal, but in any case the phrase encapsulates what this scholar-saint was all about.

F · O · U · R

aquinas's

summa theologica

POPE Leo XIII in his 1879 encyclical *Aeterni Patris* officially confirmed Thomas Aquinas as the greatest theologian of the Catholic Church. "Reason, reared aloft on the wings of Saint Thomas, could scarcely soar higher, and it is almost impossible even for faith to be supported by additional or stronger aids from reason than has been furnished by the Angelic Doctor." Thomas wrote voluminously in his forty-nine years, but no single text distills his supreme wisdom more completely than the *Summa Theologica*, composed between 1265 and 1273.

For the average person, the *Summa* is virtually an unreadable document. It is more than 1,000 pages long and contains 38 tracts, 631 questions, and 3,000 articles, in which more than 10,000 objections to Thomas's position are laboriously refuted. Thomas knew the Scriptures almost by heart, and fluently quotes from them throughout his text; in addition there are references to 19 Catholic councils, 41 popes, 52 Fathers of the Church or Doctors, and 346 classical philosophers such as Plato and Aristotle. Given this staggering breadth, it is almost unbelievable that Aquinas wrote his *Summa* as an introductory manual for theology students. With characteristic understatement, Thomas noted that "beginners in this sacred science are very much impeded by the multiplication of useless questions, articles, and arguments": hence, this book as a sort of mild corrective.

In the opinion of many philosophers, there has never been — and is not likely to be — a single work which better defends Catholic orthodoxy, which does more credit to the Middle Ages, which more incisively and completely addresses the basic questions of philosophy, which erects as towering and majestic a theological edifice, as the *Summa*. This book represents reason at its best. It is never sneering, although it is combating dangerous heresy; it is meticulously organized, moving from proofs of God's existence to his attributes to his creation to our attributes; it gives fair play to arguments against its position, and then answers them; it draws on the widest possible range of sources, from the Bible to the Greeks to the Arabian thinkers to the Manicheans to Neoplatonist theologians; finally, it shows a tremendous balance in its equal emphasis on soul and body, faith and intellect, freedom and order.

There is even a good reason for the *Summa* being boring. It's not because Thomas couldn't write with feeling — he composed several hymns with moving lyrics, and toward the end of his life he had mystical experiences. But he also believed, with his favorite author Aristotle, that poetry and good writing often confused the issues and substituted emotion for good judgment. Thus his format was deliberately dry and antiseptic: he stated his proposition, then invoked authorities in support of it, then listed refutations of his view, then replied to those refutations, then summarized his conclusion.

It would seem, from all this, that Thomas led a rather dull life. Actually, from a physical as well as intellectual standpoint, his life was extremely adventurous. He was born in the county of Aquino near Naples around 1225. His mother was a Norman, his father a Lombard. At the age of only five, they sent Thomas to the Abbey of Monte Cassino as an oblate. They wanted the prestige of having their son become a Benedictine monk, perhaps eventually head of a monastery. But around 1239, Thomas — even then of independent mind — announced to his family his decision to join the Dominicans, a mendicant, or begging, order. This outraged his parents and brothers, who tried to reason with him; but that failing, they kidnapped him and kept him for a year in Roccasecca, the family castle. Lack of food failed to persuade the boy, so his brothers sent him a sexy, half-clad maiden to arouse his passions. This was just too much — the otherwise immobile Thomas leaped from his seat and, seizing a firebrand, drove the screaming girl out of his room. Eventually, his family relented and released Thomas, who promptly signed up with the Dominicans.

He received a superb education which he absorbed with his great intellect. Later when asked what he was most thankful to God for, he replied, "I have understood every page I have ever read." He studied at the Imperial University of Naples, where the renowned Peter of Ireland lectured on Aristotle. In 1245, he went to the University of Paris, where his teacher was Albert the Great, perhaps the best-known theologian in Europe at the time. Curiously, Thomas had a reputation for being inward and rather dull. This owed itself to his huge head, bulky frame, and dreamy manner — he seemed in a different world, anchored to this one only because of his physical size. At one point, Albert the Great scolded some students who had nicknamed Thomas "Dumb Ox." Thundered Albert, "You call him a Dumb Ox. I tell you this

Dumb Ox shall bellow so loud that his bellowings will fill the world."

Albert was to have an enormous influence on Thomas; in fact, in 1248 Aquinas would follow his teacher to Cologne, where Albert wanted to found a house of studies for the Dominican order. And Thomas would complete the intellectual venture which occupied Albert throughout his life, but which Albert did not have the ability to fully handle: the synthesis of the philosophy of Aristotle and the theology of Catholicism in such a way that orthodoxy was not violated.

It is difficult today to understand the importance of such a synthesis, but in the thirteenth century it was a task of the greatest urgency. The early Middle Ages did have a rudimentary knowledge of Aristotle, but not until Aquinas's time were complete translations of most of Aristotle's works from the original Greek available to scholars. Catholic theology had relied mainly on Platonic ideas, which through Saint Augustine and others had been adequately reconciled to Church teaching. But Aristotle seemed much more intractable: he claimed the universe was eternal; he denied that God was anything other than a "first mover" of creation; his Greek humanism seemed to contrast favorably with Catholic asceticism. It shocked many medievals that here was an entire science and ethics which seemed completely nonreliant on Christian concepts. Some Catholic thinkers dismissed Aristotle as a pest and a heretic, but his knowledge of physics, astronomy, logic, ethics — his entire system of thought — was so complete, so beautiful, that he soon became impossible to ignore.

Even at the University of Paris, one of the great founts of medieval orthodoxy since it was founded by the emperor Frederick II, Catholics were being converted to

Aristotelianism. This gave rise to a very powerful stream of thought, Averroism, which maintained that there were two kinds of truths — those of reason and those of religion. Aristotle represented the former, Scripture and Church tradition the latter. Who cared if the two truths conflicted? They were like two heads on a hydra, and Catholics could believe that Aristotle was rationally right, and the Church was metaphysically right. This was the view of Siger of Brabant, the most famous of the Averroists.

It was a view repugnant to Aquinas, partly because it came so close to his own. Aquinas read Aristotle in the original translation of William of Moerbeke, and he was attracted to "The Philosopher," as he calls him in the *Summa*. Aquinas was aware that to reject Aristotle would be to reject the most comprehensive intellectual synthesis known to man. Yet his attempt to baptize Aristotle was not pragmatic. He found Aristotelian ideas useful, but only because he found them to be true. And although Thomas knew that Aristotle was not a Christian, he saw no fundamental conflict between the principles of Aristotle and the principles of Christianity. Also, he did not find Christian doctrine in the least unreasonable — indeed he believed that reason was simply a way to demonstrate conclusions which could just as easily be taken on faith from the Bible.

Three of Aristotle's main distinctions were between act and potential, between matter and form, and between substance and accident. Potential is what things are capable of becoming; act is fulfilled potential. Matter is the substance of which all things are made; form is the shape or character that distinguishes one thing from another. Substance is the thing itself; accident refers to its attributes. To this Aquinas adds his own distinction, between the nature of things or their essence, and their being or existence. With this, he is ready to bring about a revolution in Catholic thought.

He begins with the famous five proofs of God's existence. The first proof is from motion or change. Our senses tell us that there is movement or change in the world. But everything that is moved is moved by something else, and perhaps that something else in turn is moved by another mover. But this regresses to a first mover, something or someone who sets the whole process in motion. This mover we call God.

The second proof is from cause. We see in the world causes and effects; every effect has a cause. Now perhaps A is caused by B which is caused by C. This series cannot go on infinitely — if there were no first cause, there could not be a second, and so on. So there had to be a first cause, which Aquinas says is another term for God.

One caveat: when Aquinas says that "the series cannot go on infinitely" he is not thinking of a mathematical series. Of course we can have, say, a series of integers which extends indefinitely on the positive and negative side. Nor is Aquinas thinking about a series stretching backward and forward in time. Rather he means that any series — including an eternal universe — in order to have being or existence, must depend on something outside the series. Otherwise, how is it sustained? Aquinas is really saying that the movement and contingency of the world cannot be without some ultimate explanation.

The third proof is from perishability. Things exist and perish, we know from experience. Thus for each thing a time must come when it does not exist. But assuming, as Aristotle did, that the universe is eternal, probability dictates that there must have come a moment when all things were in nonexistence (that is, when nothing existed). But if nothing ever existed, then how did anything start to exist after that? There must be a necessary being, says Aquinas, which draws its existence from itself — and this is God.

The fourth proof is from degree. We notice in the world things more or less beautiful, more or less good, and so on. But these relative terms imply a standard of beauty and goodness in which the objects we refer to participate to a lesser or greater degree. Thus there must exist a being which establishes the standard of beauty, goodness, and all other perfections, a being who is God.

The fifth proof is from order. We observe in the universe an astonishing harmony. Nature seems ordered unto herself, and "we see things which lack knowledge act for an end, which is clear from the fact that they act in the same way," Aquinas writes. But this suggests an intelligence or plan at work; we cannot assume the order is random. If we came across a beautifully made clock, working perfectly, we would automatically assume a clockmaker. This then, is God — the clockmaker of the universe. The German philosopher Immanuel Kant greatly admired this proof.

Aquinas's proofs, and indeed his entire philosophical system, start from sense-experience. In this he contrasts markedly with Plato, and with Saint Augustine who was in the Platonic tradition. Reading those two you sometimes got the sense that all that mattered was the soul, that the body was an inconvenient appendage — base matter for the soul to discipline and govern.

Augustine also distrusted the intellect, placing virtually all his emphasis on faith. Aquinas agreed that faith or revealed truth is always supreme. He also admitted that most people, at most times, don't act by reason —

they act by faith and habit. In the *Summa* Aquinas says that the truth about God is arrived at by reason "only by very few men and after a long time and with the admixture of many errors." In that sense reason is aristocratic, faith democratic. And yet Aquinas believed that faith and reason never contradict each other, that it was possible to arrive at truths about God through intellect. If not, why did God create the intellect? Aquinas says that God gave us our body and our senses to experience the truth of God, and our minds to make sense of that experience.

By coincidence Aquinas taught at the University of Paris across the hall from another great theologian, Bonaventure (canonized in 1482). Thomas had studied three years under Albert the Great at Cologne; then he returned to Paris and lectured on the *Sentences* of Peter Lombard, after which he received his license to teach theology. Bonaventure became a professor about the same time, but he had an entirely different outlook than Aquinas. Bonaventure was a Franciscan and a poet; Thomas was a Dominican and a philosopher. Franciscans valued revelation and despised reason; Dominicans valued both. A good deal of the internecine conflict within Catholicism during that time was between these two powerful streams of thought. The Franciscans opposed all efforts to "baptize" Aristotle because they felt this would have the effect of diluting and compromising Christianity. They believed Plato's ideas looked forward to Christian revelation for their consummation. But they regarded Aristotle as a naturalistic thinker fundamentally opposed to Christianity. It is easy to see how Aquinas, much against his will, was drawn into the controversy.

What Aquinas resented was that his motives were being questioned. Admittedly, he was an admirer of Aristotle, but he was a devotee of Christ. Where Aristotle differed from Catholic orthodoxy Thomas brilliantly showed how Aristotle had reasoned incorrectly from his own premises — these premises, in fact, led directly to the Catholic understanding. Aquinas did not dilute, but enrich, Christianity with Aristotelian concepts.

Fortunately Aquinas said all these things with humility. And though an intellectual giant, he was an unassuming, even self-deprecating, man. Just as he joined a mendicant order rather than seek a high post at a monastery, so also he chose Aristotle over Plato because Aristotle's ideas were closer to real-life experience. God can be known from his works, Saint Paul tells us in his Letter to the Romans. Aristotle wrote not about abstracts but about things people could see and touch. In this Aquinas saw a latent Christian humility and a latent Christian specificity. Plato was impersonal and unspecific. But Christianity was not — its entire doctrine rested on the God who became man, who worked as a carpenter and was nailed to a tree. And most Christians didn't worship God through Platonic forms flying about in the sky; they worshiped with their bodies, with their hands outstretched, and with their hearts.

Thomas's humility — and his sense of humor — came through when somebody wrote him asking whether the names of all the saints were written on a scroll publicly exhibited in heaven. Thomas replied patiently, "So far as I can see, this is not the case, but there is no harm in saying so."

In the long run, it is Thomas's self-effacing approach to Aristotle which saved him. As Chesterton wrote, "It was precisely because his Catholicism was so convincing that his Aristotelianism was given the benefit of the doubt." Not at first: Aristotle's *Physics* and *Metaphysics* were banned by the Church in 1215; thanks to

Aquinas's criticism, the Averroistic philosophy of Siger of Brabant was repeatedly condemned; unfortunately, in 1277, Bishop Stephen Tempier of Paris issued a denunciation of two hundred nineteen Averroistic theses but included twenty Thomistic propositions. But later this condemnation of Thomas would be reversed by Bishop Tempier's successor, and all trace of doubt would be removed in 1323, when Aquinas would be made a saint.

The *Summa Theologica*, unlike Aquinas's other great work *Summa Contra Gentiles*, is primarily a work of philosophy. It starts from proofs of God and then goes on to examine what this God is like and what he has created. In discussing the attributes of God Aquinas suggests that we begin by identifying negative attributes — things God is not — because God's essence exceeds the human mind's ability to grasp it. Hopefully, by eliminating possibilities we will arrive at some understanding of our Maker.

From the first proof of God based on motion, we saw that God was the First Mover. This implies that God does not change; he has no beginning or end; he is eternal. As God is eternal he is never in potency — with unrealized possibilities; hence, God must be pure act. But if God is pure act, then God cannot be composed of matter, because matter is defined as always in potency. So God is immaterial; he is spirit.

Then Aquinas turns to God's positive attributes. He reminds us that we can only speak "analogically" here, because human beings and things have attributes — we get these from God. God, on the other hand, does not have attributes; he embodies them. Thus when we say God is "good," we do mean that he is the source of all human goodness, but we do not mean that God's goodness is simply human goodness of infinite magnitude.

Aquinas gives an example to illustrate this: health. An animal is healthy, he says, because it is the subject of health; it possesses health. Medicine is also said to be healthy, but for a different reason: it causes health. A girl is said to have a healthy complexion because her complexion shows signs of health. So the word "health" is used in different though similar senses to refer to different things.

By the same token, when we speak of God's goodness we mean goodness in a different sense than human goodness. There is a comparison, based on resemblance, between human goodness and divine goodness, but the two are not identical. After all, in God, all perfections — goodness, justice, compassion, etc. — are not distinct, either from each other or from the divine essence. In man they are.

Can there be more than one God? No, answers Aquinas, because God is perfection, and if there were several perfect beings there would be nothing to distinguish them, and they would all merge into one. So God is one, and he is unique. He is also all-powerful, drawing his power from his essence. Are there things God cannot do? Yes, a few. God cannot will his own nonexistence. God cannot create a being that simultaneously has, and does not have, reason. But these are not "things" at all; they are contradictions in terms. There is essentially no limit to God's power.

What about evil? Taking a cue from Augustine, Aquinas argues that evil is a deprivation; it has no separate existence. This does not mean evil cannot have tangible effects. It does mean evil does not have "being." In fact, evil is the lack of a good quality; for example, a greedy man is one who does not possess contentment. God cannot be blamed for creating evil because evil has no separate existence; it is even, in a sense, dependent on a corresponding good.

Human beings are not created out of nothing, Aquinas argues, but out of God. Our existence derives from his. If we were simply created *ex nihilo*, we would be independent beings, but we are not. We are contingent beings; our every breath is drawn with God's permission. This, however, does not mean we do not have free will — the will is unconstrained; we are even at liberty to reject God.

Aquinas believed that he could prove the existence of angels. They are nothing but pure intellect, he said. Invoking the Aristotelian hierarchical conception of the universe, Aquinas notes that animals are pure body and no real intellect; man is both body and intellect; he infers that there must logically be created beings who have no body but do have intellect. Angels only fulfill the continuum of beings created by God. And as for that old medieval conundrum — how many angels can dance on the point of a pin? — the answer is "an infinite number," because angels don't have bodies and don't take up space.

Souls of humans are on a slightly lower plane than angels, Aquinas says. The angel, like the soul, is composed of potency and act; in both, essence differs from existence; both are pure form, without admixture of matter. But the soul has a lesser intellect than the angel, and thus it is capable of merging with the body to form a human being. How can the "base" matter of the body mix with the "pure" intellect of the soul? The body should not be considered base or evil, Aquinas argues; if it were evil it would not exist. Soul and body complement each other, he says.

We see from this the central importance of existence in Aquinas's philosophy. Everything that exists is created by God, and it is good. That which is bad does not really exist — it lacks being. And as for God, in him essence and existence are one. Aquinas believed that the most appropriate name of God is the one God gave Moses at the burning bush, "I Am Who Am." God's nature is his being. Human beings, by contrast, have their own nature, but they draw their existence from God.

Thomas even attempts to explain such difficult and mysterious notions as the transubstantiation. We are puzzled, Aquinas notes, because we do not see the bread and wine change into the body and blood of Christ at the Eucharist; at least, our senses are unable to perceive that anything has happened. But this is not surprising, Aquinas says. Things are divided into substance and accident. Substance is immaterial — it is that by virtue of which a thing is; accidents are that by virtue of which a thing can be changed. There is no visual change in the bread and wine because it is their substance which is changed into the substance of the body and blood of Christ. In other words there has been a transfer of being, although the outward attributes remain the same.

What about that peculiarly Catholic notion of purgatory? Aquinas says it is a place for souls to build up ascetical discipline before getting to heaven. The trauma of purgatory, he writes, is not the hellish sense of total loss, but impatience. Souls are restless to reach God for eternal bliss; they are just dying to get to God, so to speak. One day they will be reunited with him.

This is only a glimpse of Thomas's great theological edifice, but hopefully it suggests how the Angelic Doctor is able to work out implications of his theorems, and fit things together in a consistent and orderly manner. Medieval thinking — which sometimes confused reason and revelation — sorely needed this synthesis.

Aquinas spent his whole life spreading the Christian message in its most lucid and comprehensible form. In his short life of forty-nine years, he traveled a great deal — he was famous in Paris at all the universities; he had lectured at Naples, Rome, and Lyons; he almost certainly visited London: this at a time when most people spent their lives within a radius of a few miles from their birthplace. To say he wrote prolifically would be an understatement; he left literally bales of manuscripts which would occupy the transcribing time of monks for years and years after his death. Yet his more than one hundred lengthy works show a closely textured reasoning and creative thinking — he never sacrificed quality for quantity. He also used his persuasive powers to serve his Church. At Pope Urban's request, he reviewed the text of an Italian bishop attempting the difficult but necessary task of reconciling Eastern- and Western-rite Catholicism. The pope also asked Aquinas to edit various commentaries of Greek and Latin Fathers on the four Gospels.

Throughout his years Aquinas was eminently reasonable, but he never forgot the limitations of reason. In fact, in December of 1273, while saying Mass, he had a mystical experience which caused him to suspend work on the third part of the *Summa Theologica*. He told his secretary he was at the end of his writing; in fact, "Compared to what has been revealed to me, all that I have written seems to me like so much straw."

In 1274, Aquinas was summoned by Pope Gregory X to attend the Council of Lyons, which would attempt a reconciliation between Rome and the Greek Church; but Aquinas fell ill on the way, and died at his sister's house at Fossanuova. As he received the last rites, he prayed to his Maker, "I receive you, ransom of my soul. For love of you have I studied and kept vigil, toiled, preached, and taught."

Thomas Aquinas was no more, but his ideas would live on. They have had an enormous effect on religious thinking ever since. First they have affected doctrine; for instance, Aquinas's insistence that man is composed not just of soul or of body, but of soul *and* body, was defined as a dogma of the faith at the Council of Vienne in 1311. Aquinas set Catholic theology on an entirely new course, and he gave it a basis in reason which enabled not just Catholics, but all serious philosophers, to consider it on its merits. Thanks to Aquinas, the Dominican order developed a strong intellectual mindset. As early as 1259 Aquinas attended his order's general chapter meeting at Valendiennes, where it was decided that a philosophy course would be required of seminarians. This intellectual rigor enabled Catholicism to defend itself against future assaults from philosophers who refused to accept its revealed truths. Finally there is an extensive catalog of people in all fields who have been influenced by Aquinas — such diverse figures as Dante, James Joyce, Étienne Gilson and Jacques Maritain (two of the greatest Thomist philosophers), John Courtney Murray, Karl Rahner, T.S. Eliot, and American politician Eugene McCarthy.

There are those who say that Saint Thomas Aquinas was the most luminous mind the world has ever known. The Angelic Doctor would cringe at this description. Throughout his life he tried to draw attention to ideas, and to Christ, and to draw attention away from himself. Such greatness and such humility seldom go together.

dante's

divine comedy

ALONG with Homer's *Iliad* and Milton's *Paradise Lost*, the *Divine Comedy* of Dante Alighieri represents the very pinnacle of poetic accomplishment. Never have intellect and imagination come together in a more inspiring synthesis; never has the soul soared higher. Yet aesthetic beauty is buttressed by moral purpose. Just as Milton set himself the task of "justifying the ways of God to man," so one of Dante's goals in writing the *Comedy* is to "cause people to pray." The poem shows us the whole course of religious conversion.

It is not as easy to analyze the *Comedy* bit by bit as it is to dissect, say, the *Summa Theologica*. That is because the former is a poem, the latter is mainly philosophy. Philosophy does not suffer when it is broken down into component parts; by contrast, poems are like moonbeams — you can admire each shimmering strand of color, but the whole is greater than the sum of the parts.

To reach his goal, Dante draws not only on the range of Christian philosophy but also on Greek and Latin poetry. He invokes Scripture, but just as often he quotes the classical poet Virgil, and he is not averse to including contemporary poets and political figures of Florence in his celestial scheme. Oddly enough, his guide through the Christian schema of hell and purgatory is Virgil, the pagan poet who wrote the *Aeneid*.

Mysteries abound in the *Divine Comedy*. Why are so many Italian politicians in hell? Why is heaven filled with Romans who presumably never had a chance to accept Christ? Is this really a story of Dante's journey through the inferno and up to God? If so, is this a literal or a spiritual journey? Can there really be popes in hell? Who is the woman known as Beatrice, and why is it her prerogative to take Dante to the inner circle of heaven, the empyrean? These questions cannot be answered without reference to Dante's life on earth.

Dante Alighieri was born into an ancient Florentine family in 1265. His father was a banker who hated Christianity — he died a heretic when Dante was fifteen. His mother, Bella, died even earlier, so Dante was raised by his stepmother and sisters. He was always a rebellious and proud youth; his famous biographer Boccaccio would describe him as one "of lofty and scornful disposition." He learned to hunt, fence, dance, play music, and ride horses, all at an early age. He particularly loved classical and courtly poetry, and at age eighteen, he wrote his first love song.

But his first romantic attachment occurred at the astonishingly precocious age of nine. He was captivated by one Beatrice Portinari, a lovely lass in his neighborhood, age eight. It might strike us as bizarre that this youthful adulation should form the basis for Dante's mature poetry. After all, nothing happened between Dante and Beatrice; in fact, both she and Dante ended up marrying other people, and Beatrice died at the age of twenty-four in 1290.

Yet it was precisely because Dante's love was unfulfilled that it remained eternal. Like the frozen figures in Keats's *Ode to a Grecian Urn*, the man would forever pursue the maiden with no hope of ever catching her. Beatrice's death sent Dante into a period of inconsolable mourning. His whole world was changed before his eyes. Even lively Florence, bustling with industry and political intrigue (which Dante loved), suddenly seemed cold and desolate. Dante's wife, Gemma Donati, bore him two children, whom he dearly loved, but they could not mitigate his grief.

This grief was spiritual in nature. In his teens Dante may have lusted for Beatrice, but after her death she only came to symbolize perfection — beauty, truth, all those eternal "forms" which Plato defined as transmitting virtues to things of this world. In the *Divine Comedy* Beatrice is the woman herself — pristine and lovely — but she is also a symbol for God's love; that is why she can fix her unblinking eye on the Creator, why she sits on a throne along with Rachel in the heavenly circle of the Mystic Rose.

Shortly after Beatrice's death Dante went searching for a new lady to console him, and he found one — the Lady Philosophy. This lady had also consoled Boethius as he awaited his execution; indeed Dante is familiar with Boethius's *Consolation of Philosophy* which influenced him very much. He stops composing love poetry and, around 1304-1308, writes the *Convivio*, an autobiographical work with a philosophical tone.

Philosophy by herself is unable to console Dante, as it did Boethius, and his soul remains restive. Unfortunately this is compounded by the destruction of his career. Dante belonged to a political party or clan called the Guelfs, which were in power in Florence at the time. In 1289, Dante fought victoriously for the Guelf rulers of

Florence against invaders at Campaldino. But the Guelf party split into what were called White Guelfs and Black Guelfs. The Black Guelfs formed an alliance with Pope Boniface VIII and ousted the White Guelfs; as a result, Dante was sent into exile on trumped-up charges of financial corruption and conspiracy against the pope, launched by Corso Donati, a member of his wife's own family. Dante was to spend the rest of his life separated from his loved ones and his country.

So the *Divine Comedy* was not written in the best of times for young Alighieri. It is therefore significant that it is a comedy — that it has a happy ending — instead of a tragedy. Despite his troubles, Dante realized that he was part of the moral order of the universe, and his Creator had a special plan in store for him. "God writes no tragedies," as one commentator put it. In fact, Dante's lost dreams led him to a broader vision of things not material which mattered. As for his career, it would never be restored; but he would get his Beatrice back — and she would escort him to heaven, where he would be one with his Maker.

Interestingly, the *Comedy* is written in the vernacular, not in Latin. Why choose a parochial tongue — Italian — when Dante could use the great Church script? Dante suggests that it is because our mother tongue is what we receive from nature; Latin is what we receive from art. He is writing an epic, true; but he is writing a Christian epic, and what is epic about Christianity is not its grandeur but its humility. So it is right that Dante should use his mother tongue so that he can speak from the heart.

The *Comedy* begins on the eve of Good Friday in the year 1300, when Dante sets foot into hell. It will take him until the morning of Easter Sunday to reach purgatory, and three days later he will be in paradise — though the flight through the circles of heaven will be timeless. These dates are important because Dante is suggesting that he is making the same journey that Christ did when, after his crucifixion, "he descended into hell and on the third day rose again."

The poem is divided into three main sections — inferno, purgatory, and paradise. Each section is divided into thirty-three cantos. Along with the introductory canto this makes one hundred cantos in all: the perfect number. Notice, also, Dante's preference for the number three, which is the number of the Trinity. Throughout the *Comedy* there is a tremendous symmetry, but this does not seem to place constraints upon the poet; rather, it further elevates the poem, because the tumultuous urges of the soul and the immeasurable love of the Almighty are structured into a carefully controlled verse, so there is a pleasing contrast between the form of the *Comedy* and its content.

Dante adopts a Ptolemaic universe, upon which he improvises, for the geographical layout of his poem. Hell is located at the center of the universe; it is a funnel of ever-widening circles with Jerusalem at its apex. The mountain of purgatory rises out of the other side of the world. The idea is that God hurled Satan, the defiant angel, toward earth, and as the devil plowed through its surface, he churned up land at the other end, which formed the purgatorial mountain. So the fall of the angels provided for man the chance for purification even before the sin of Adam and Eve. The concentric circles of paradise lie outside the earth — they end in the empyrean, which is in another realm altogether, outside them. Quite a journey for Dante to make, as we shall see.

The *Inferno* begins with Dante "in a dark wood

where the straight way was lost." He has sinned, and he feels bitter. At this low point a ghostly figure appears — it is Virgil. Dante recognizes him; he tells Dante he has been sent by Beatrice. "Love moved me and makes me speak," Virgil says. He means both love in the literal sense (Beatrice's love) and love as a metonymy for divine love, divine grace. It is appropriate that Virgil be Dante's guide because one of his poems, the fourth eclogue, forecasts the incarnation of Christ.

There is another reason for Virgil, the poet, as guide. Dante has to deal with the medieval opinion, most powerfully stated by Aquinas, that — to be blunt — poets are liars. They make up stories and pass them off for truth. Dante never directly answers Thomas, of course; but his poem seems to say that, in the realm of the spirit, it is just as true as anything Thomas ever wrote. In fact, Dante's view was that rationalistic abstracts sometimes turned religion into something which could no longer be felt, only defined. Perhaps, the *Comedy* seems to say, the idea of God as a white-haired loving father is more "true" than the idea of God as some sort of uncaused being. As a poet, Virgil can demonstrate spiritual truths to Dante in a way that perhaps a philosopher could not.

At the gateway of hell is emblazoned the famous sign, "Abandon all hope, ye that enter here." That is what makes hell so unbearable; it leads nowhere; it is eternal torment; there is no hope. On the perimeter of hell, Dante and Virgil see the neutrals — those lukewarm souls who never sided either with evil or righteousness. Dante keeps them nameless — after all, their lives amounted to nothing — and they march behind a banner, stung by hornets.

Charon, the white-haired old man, steers the two men across the swirling dark current of the river

Acheron, into the first circle of hell. There Dante recognizes the "virtuous heathen": those noble souls who never recognized Christ, but whom Dante loved and admired. Plato, Aristotle, Cicero, Seneca, Euclid, Ptolemy — they are all here; even fictional characters, such as Hector and Aeneas, inhabit this circle, which is characterized by a terrible mournfulness.

The second circle contains Paolo and Francesca, whose story is perhaps the most touching in the entire *Comedy*. Their sin was illicit love, and thus they are buffeted about by a powerful wind; but even in their misery, they "cling together like doves." Francesca pleads with Dante that she is not responsible for her sin; she was trapped by "love, which absolves no one from loving." Dante, filled with pity for the young lovers, swoons "and falls, even as a dead body falls."

History soils the story of Paolo and Francesca a bit. It turns out that she was married to a cripple and fell in love with his virile brother. But she already had a nine-year-old daughter and he was a forty-year-old man with two children when their affair took place. Somehow, that takes them out of the class of Helen of Troy, Tristan, and Dido, all of whom are in this second circle of hell for sins of lust. But Dante's Paolo and Francesca are not the historical Paolo and Francesca, and as such they are symbols for young hearts who refuse to accept the bounds of love. Modern commentators have pooh-poohed the idea that a loving God would send two passionate creatures like Paolo and Francesca to hell — their love seems too complete, even sacred. But it is because love is sacred that it must be distinguished from lust — and Paolo and Francesca's failure to make this distinction is their undoing. Their story remains tragic, but Dante feels their fate is deserved.

In the third circle of gluttony, Dante and Virgil encounter the emblem of greed itself, the monster Cerberus, whom Dante describes as having "red eyes, a beard greasy and black, a great belly, and clawed hands" with which he scars and rips the gluttonous souls wallowing in the filth and the rain. One of these is the fat Ciacco, whose name means "hog"; he was a well-known eater in Florence during Dante's time, and Florentines would be much amused to see someone they knew, good old Ciacco, writhing in hell. Ciacco is not, of course, the last contemporary of Dante that our poet will discover in the depths of the inferno.

In fact, in the fifth circle, Dante finds one of his political opponents, Filip Argenti, who is being punished for the sin of wrath. Argenti pleads with Dante, but the poet is completely indifferent; in fact, he wants to kick Argenti back into the mud, and cheers when the suffering Argenti is beaten by other angry souls in hell. This may strike the modern reader as cruel on Dante's part, and we will see such behavior again, in the depths of the ninth circle, where Dante refuses to clear the eyes of Fra Alberigo, a traitor who is incarcerated in a block of ice.

Dante's contempt for Argenti and Alberigo does not show his weakness. He is not acting in the heat of passion. Rather, he is showing respect for the just order of the universe. Argenti was a ruthless politician. Alberigo pretended to be reconciled to his brother and then ruthlessly slaughtered him. Worst of all, neither of these two repented of their sins. So Dante's indignation is justified — it parallels God's righteousness.

The sixth circle for the heretics includes a study in Italian contrasts: Guido Cavalcante, panicky as he peers around for his son; and Farinata degli Uberti, a defiant politician whose "lifted eyebrow" shows his utter scorn for Cavalcante, for Dante, for hell, even for God. As Guido grovels, Farinata is unmoved and carries on his conversation with Dante, asking him who his ancestors were and noting that "they were my fierce enemies" and "I scattered them" in battle. Dante admires Farinata, but the latter is being punished for putting his political party above his country, and above God.

As Dante is trudging through the inferno he hears a tremendous rumbling — hell itself trembles, and tumbling boulders boom everywhere. "Upon all sides the deep and loathsome valley trembled, so that I thought the universe was thrilled by love," Dante writes. Remember that this is Good Friday, and thirteen hundred years earlier, the earth shook with similar convulsions when Christ gave up his earthly life. Dante invokes the crucifixion because it is the supreme example of God's love — love which penetrates even the lower regions of hell. Dante is also reversing the ancient doctrine of Empedocles, who posited love as a unifying force in the world, and hate and discord as disorganizing powers. For Dante, hate conspires and makes rigid; love brings true freedom. You shall know love, and love will make you free, Dante is saying.

Love is at the center of the *Divine Comedy*. But it is important that it be brought up here, because in hell it is easy to forget that love exists. Dante has moved beyond the upper circles of hell, which simply punish perversions of love. Lust, sloth, extravagance, gluttony: these are sins of impulse, of desires carried too far. Even anger, discontent, and violence are passions that have not been reined. But in the inner circles we find the sins which represent a deliberate repudiation of God's love — heinous sins of blasphemy, false prophecy, the sowing of discord, and treachery.

Right at the bottom of hell, in the frozen lake, Dante sees Lucifer himself, "the creature who was once so fair." Three faces — the unholy trinity — spring out of his neck, and with his three mouths Lucifer is chewing the heads of Judas Iscariot, who betrayed Jesus, and Cassius and Brutus, who betrayed the emperor Caesar. These three traitors belong with the great betrayer himself — Satan who rebelled against God, and turned God's creation against the Maker of all things.

Out of this dark cavern, with its icy blast, come Dante and Virgil, and once again they could see the stars. From the descent into hell, they must now climb the mountain of purgatory. Purgatory is distinguished from hell not by the absence of punishment but by the presence of hope. Souls suffer here, but they suffer almost willingly: they are eager to atone for their sins so that they might stand in the sunlight of God. There are no shrieks of anguish in purgatory. Rather, the atmosphere is almost like a somber church service — brooding and dignified.

Dante himself has sinned, Beatrice tells him, so he too must cleanse himself if he is to make the trip to heaven. He has not yet learned the discipline of repentance, however; as he enters purgatory he lingers to hear the singer Casella play a hometown song. But the guardsman of purgatory, the philosopher Cato, sharply rebukes Dante, who must learn to resist the seduction of old friends and familiar music. He begins to climb, but the ascent is difficult; the souls must walk upon the path of their own sins; they must "make stepping-stones of their dead selves."

In hell, as you go deeper, the sins get worse; in purgatory, as you climb higher, the sins get lighter. Pride, envy, and anger are sins of the spirit; greed, lust, and gluttony are sins of the flesh; between these is gloom or fatalism, which often brings about faults much graver than itself. On the first terrace Dante sees, painted on the white marble wall, images of pride. Lucifer, the vain angel, is there, along with those who tried to build the Tower of Babel to reach heaven. Envy is the sister of pride; Dante gives the example of the lady Sapia, who hated her enemies and prayed for their deaths: she cried with joy when they were slain in battle. Now, of course, she is not celebrating but crying, for she recognizes her sin, and is trying to rid herself of it. She asks Dante whether he is atoning for the same sin and he says no; he runs not the risk of being envious but being proud of his poetic genius.

Dante also admits his sin when, among the gluttons in purgatory, he meets his cousin Forese Donati. They were both poets in Florence, and shared some rollicking times. "If you recall to mind what you and I were together, the present memory will still be painful," Dante tells Forese. For his sins of pride and greed Beatrice will chastise Dante when he reaches the top of the purgatory mountain. "How did you think yourself worthy to climb the mountain?" Beatrice asks. "Did you not know that man here is happy?"

Just as in hell the punishment fits the crime, so in purgatory repentance fits the sin. For example, in the inferno the gluttons are whipped with rain and stones, the slothful roll and slam against each other, and the treacherous find themselves punished with elaborate and ingenious tortures: reversed heads, serpent bodies, and bucketfuls of boiling pitch. So in purgatory, the gluttonous souls, although lean and hungry, must suffer as they stand before the branches of the tree overflowing with fruit which they cannot eat. This is man's original temptation in the garden of Eden; the souls in purgatory are being given a second chance at it, so to speak.

After Dante has passed over the terraces of the seven deadly sins, he reaches the earthly paradise, and here Virgil must leave. He did not understand the meaning of his own fourth eclogue, Dante implies: the poem was Christian, but Virgil remained to his death a pagan. So salvation must forever be denied him. Also, Virgil is a symbol of human reason, and reason can only go so far in bringing one to repentance and salvation. But the pagan poet Statius (who joined Virgil and Dante earlier) stays with Dante, and here is a remarkable fact about the *Comedy* — Dante pretends that Statius has been baptized a Christian, although there is no historical evidence for this.

From here begins the rapid ascent into heaven. If the mood of the inferno was punishment or righteousness, and the mood of purgatory was hope and discipline, paradise is definitely about love and ecstasy. The word love appears 77 times in Book III of the *Comedy*, compared to 50 times in purgatory and 19 times in hell. And while Dante entered hell at night on Friday, and purgatory at dawn on Sunday, he begins the heavenly journey at midday on Wednesday: it is the sacred hour of noon. And since there is no such thing as time in heaven, Dante's prose assumes a dazzling pace. He seems caught up in whirls of divine power, as he is hurled upward to the fountain of God's love.

The seven planets of heaven stand for the four cardinal and three theological virtues. Prudence glows in the sun, and here Dante discovers the Christian men of wisdom: Thomas Aquinas and Saint Bonaventure. But we also find two apparent heretics: Siger of Brabant and Joachim of Flora. And Siger and Aquinas, bitter adversaries during their lifetimes, are standing together; so are the rivals Joachim and Bonaventure. Dante seems to suggest that all these men contributed to wisdom and we should not judge errors committed in an attempt to clarify the Catholic faith as heresy.

On the planet Mercury, we find the emperor Justinian. Here Dante introduces the idea that Justinian, and other emperors, are directly appointed by God. This notion of the "divine right of kings" will become commonplace in Europe, but during the Middle Ages, it was considered radical. Thomas Aquinas, for example, held that the king's power must be subordinate to the power of the Catholic Church. But Dante believed that Church and State had totally separate domains, and for attempting to break down the wall of separation, Pope Boniface VIII finds himself placed by Dante in the inferno.

Venus stands for love, and here we have a surprise. In this heavenly circle, Dante finds Cunizza da Romano, the sister of a tyrant and well known for her uncontrollable lust, and Rahab the harlot. Why should these sluts be in heaven while Francesca, a woman whose love seems purer, remains in hell? Dante suggests that Cunizza and Rahab, despite their graver sins, were sorry for them, while Paolo and Francesca continue to cling to each other — still defying God's law. At least Cunizza spent her last years ministering to the sick. The point is that failure to repent, more than sin, leads to damnation.

Mars stands for fortitude, and is appropriately filled with military music. There is a ruddy glow all over the planet: this is heroism achieved through sacrifice. Dante greets Joshua, Charlemagne, and his Florentine friend Cacciaguida. In Jupiter, the planet of justice, we find more pagans, the emperor Trajan and Ripheus, along with David, Hezekiah, and Constantine — the first Roman emperor to convert to Christianity. The explanation for the pagan presence seems to be Dante's belief that their passion for justice was such a strong Christian trait that God's grace must have reached them somehow.

Self-restraint and temperance find their place in Saturn, where Dante encounters Saint Benedict, the sixth-century monk whose famous rule governed the monasteries of the early Middle Ages, and Peter Damian, the eleventh-century mystic. Dante seems to value the mystical experience above the intellect — hence Benedict and Damian occupy higher circles than Aquinas.

And the highest honor of all is reserved for another great mystic, Saint Bernard, the twelfth-century abbot of Clairvaux, who escorts the poet up the golden ladder through the fixed stars and primum mobile all the way to the empyrean — where God reigns. Here Dante experiences a sweetness that is beyond description, and as Dante comes into the light of the sun, the light of God, he is completely blinded. He is standing before the Godhead, "the love that moves the sun and the stars."

When he can see again, he realizes that all around him is music and light. Beatrice shows him the celestial rose, where the names of the saved are transcribed, and the garden of the saints, where rays of Christ shine and melody is in the air. Dante feels a tremendous contentment and finally understands what he heard earlier, "His will is our peace." These are the best-known lines in the book, and reflect Dante's belief that the restless soul finds true liberty when it brings itself into line with the will of God.

The *Divine Comedy* is a difficult poem to read because of its myriad references. But to understand it is to experience something that goes beyond the joys of experience. The reader, through Dante, gets what one Dante scholar calls "a foretaste of heaven."

Dante spent the last years of his life in exile in Ravenna. He did have a chance to come home, but only if he paid a fine and went through a shameful recantation. This Dante refused to do. He did briefly nourish hopes that a new Roman emperor, Henry VII, would take over Florence and bring about a reunion of the Holy Empire; but when Henry caught malaria and died, Dante's hopes were in tatters. Dante Alighieri died a broken man in 1321. But he left behind more for future generations than perhaps any man after Aquinas.

pascal's

pensées

ALTHOUGH the Middle Ages showed twin currents of rationalist and spiritualist thought, embodied, for example, in Thomas Aquinas and Bonaventure, Renaissance thinkers dismissed the entire millennium from A.D. 500 to 1500 as one of cold, boring rationalism. Pascal wanted to rescue Christianity from this reputation of "Scholasticism," not only to make it more palatable to seventeenth-century people, but also because he did not think that scholasticism by itself represented the Catholic faith.

"The heart has reasons which the head knows not." This famous line from Pascal, in a sense, represents his entire philosophy. He rejected a Christianity which was bogged down in arcane distinctions, which placed ritual over experience, reason over revelation, the letter of Scripture over its spirit. In this sense, Pascal took up where Saint Francis and Saint Bonaventure left off. He felt that Christ was best experienced not through some exegetical text, but through a wild impulsive leap of the heart — through faith.

This was very unusual stuff, because of its source. Pascal was not some medieval monk spouting outdated doctrines in the modern age. Rather he was one of the most brilliant scientists of all time; this gave him credibility in an age where science was revered for its potential to solve all human problems. That is why Catholicism owes a debt to this towering physicist and mathematician: just when people were beginning to think that science had refuted religion, the greatest scientist of his time stood up to dispute this, and to offer a brilliant defense of the Catholic religion.

Blaise Pascal was born in 1623 in Clermont, France, the son of a government servant. He lost his mother at age three, and was raised by two sisters and his father. In 1631, the family moved to Paris, where Pascal studied under his father's tutelage. He was a precocious learner and is said to have discovered Euclid's first thirty-two propositions on his own at the age of twelve. In the year 1640, Étienne Pascal was appointed commissioner of taxes and he and his children moved to Rouen.

Pascal's upbringing was uneventful and he was rather sickly, so it is surprising that he wrote with such verve and gusto. He was always a pale youth, excessively coddled by his sisters. He developed an aversion to this, and would later make a peculiar argument against caressing, on the grounds that eventually "the object of my attachment will die," and thus, "I should direct all my affection to him who lives forever, God." This of course, fails to recognize that love for God and love for other people are not mutually exclusive; indeed our love for fellow beings is simply a reflection of God's love in us.

Having few friends in school, Pascal spent his time thinking and writing. He published his first book at age seventeen in 1640, a mathematical treatise on cones. It was the first of many first-rate geometrical works, and indeed mathematics formed the basis for his seminal study of probabilities, and would lead to his design of calculating machines and an omnibus service, precursors of our modern computer and public transportation. The year 1640 is an important one in Pascal's life, because that same year, Cornelius Jansenius, bishop of Ypres, published his *Augustinus*. This work would become the basis for the Jansenist faith, to which Pascal would be accused of converting, even though he remained a loyal Catholic.

Pascal was attracted to Jansenism, and in feuds between the Jansenists and the Jesuits he took the side of the former, regarding the latter as truly evil. Jansenism basically holds that human nature was so thoroughly polluted by the fall that man is incapable, by himself, of attaining salvation. Man is completely dependent on the grace of God for redemption, and even then he is too conceited and stubborn to accept it — he needs grace for that too. This grace cannot be earned by good works, the Jansenists held, but man can try to remove some of the barriers to grace and thus create an atmosphere more favorable to its reception.

This doctrine was not very far from that of the Augustinians, the followers of Saint Augustine, who believed that grace was central, that very few were chosen for salvation, that austerity and self-mortification did not bring about redemption but were "signs" of being chosen for redemption. It is easy to see how all this would form the basis for the Protestant rebellion against the Catholic Church on the grounds that Catholics had substituted "good works" for "grace" as the means of reaching heaven.

There is no evidence that Pascal was a member of the Jansenist sect; in fact, he and his family were churchgoing Catholics who received the sacraments. And Pascal's *Pensées*, or *Meditations*, is a conscious effort to set forth his beliefs in complete harmony with Catholic doctrine and teaching.

In 1654, Pope Innocent III issued a condemnation of five propositions of Jansenism which were distilled from the *Augustinus* and submitted to Rome by indignant Jesuits. Many Jansenists protested the papal censure by arguing that these five propositions did not accurately reflect their beliefs, nor were they contained in Bishop Cornelius's book. They begged Pascal, a friend who made retreats with them at Port Royal des Champs, to speak out on their behalf.

The Provincial Letters, a theological dropkick aimed at the Jesuits, appeared in 1656, and in a few months they caused a storm of controversy. Pascal was not a man of understatement, and his sharp rhetorical attacks brought cries of "unfair" and "heresy" from Jesuit quarters. Unfortunately this effort drained Pascal of much of his strength. He grew paler and developed a tubercular cough. He never finished his series of letters; in fact, the nineteenth letter breaks off in mid-sentence.

The *Pensées*, Pascal's masterpiece, contains Jansenist elements, but it is an orthodox work. The tone is completely different from the *Letters*, which are fiercely polemical. In fact, Pascal in the *Pensées* seems to return to an earlier period in his life, the year 1654, when — on the "night of fire" — he had a personal revelation of Christ which transformed his life. He was sitting in his balcony when it happened; he saw what he calls "the hidden God" and he set down his experience on a piece of parchment that he carried on his person for the rest of his life. This is the mindset of *Pensées*, inspirational and devotional.

The book is both easy and difficult to read. It is easy because it contains numbered sections and paragraphs on different themes; it is possible to turn to any page and find a fresh array of insights. Yet this strength is also a weakness; the book lacks continuity, and would irk the reader who prefers a slow, unfolding argument to flashes of genius. The explanation for the structure is simple: *Pensées* was not planned as a book at all, but rather as preliminary notes for a future book which Pascal never wrote, *Apology for the Christian Religion*. Given the range and power of Pascal's observations in *Pensées*, atheists are lucky that Pascal died before he could synthesize them into his *Apology*.

A main theme throughout the *Pensées* is the deceptiveness of human reason. "Man is nothing but a subject full of natural error that cannot be eradicated except through grace," Pascal says. "Nothing shows him the truth. Everything deceives him. The two principles of truth, reason and the senses, are not only both false, but are engaged in mutual deception." The cause for this is that often the senses deceive through false appearances — we see an oasis, but it is only a mirage. And if we base our deductions on these false premises, naturally we arrive at the wrong conclusions.

Pascal is an enemy of the skeptics, who are denounced throughout the book; but in one important respect, he agrees with them: truth cannot be proved through reason alone. "Let us then concede to the skeptics what they have often proclaimed, that truth lies beyond our scope and is an unattainable quarry, that it is no earthly denizen, but at home in heaven, lying in the lap of God, to be known only insofar as it pleases him to reveal it."

This sounds a bit strong, and surely Aquinas would take issue with it. But remember that Pascal is writing at a time when reason was held to be the end-all of knowledge, when empirical science was thought to govern all truths — even concerning religion. "Knowledge is power," Francis Bacon's phrase, became the slogan of the age, and by knowledge was meant the experience of the senses then subjected to the inductive powers of the mind. Absolute knowledge, which was absolute power, did not lie in some outdated notion of God but in the scientific method in its purest form.

We have some outbursts against this sort of rationalism from Pascal, but he is not against reason per se. He identifies "two excesses: to exclude reason, and to admit nothing but reason." Some Christians want to renounce passions and become gods, he says; others want to renounce reason and become brute beasts. Both are wrong.

The point Pascal wishes to make is that reason is competent in spiritual matters only up to a point. If it does not recognize its limits and rushes madly forward, then reason only results in distortions and contradictions. "Reason's last step is the recognition that there are an infinite number of things which are beyond it," Pascal says. He also makes the point that Socrates makes in Plato's *Republic*, that true reason is, in a sense, knowledge that one is ignorant: "Knowledge has two extremes which meet. One is the pure natural ignorance of every man at birth; the other is the extreme reached by great minds who run through the whole range of human knowledge, only to find that they know nothing and come back to the same ignorance from which they set out, but it is a wise ignorance that knows itself."

True reason leads us to the recognition that we are wretched, Pascal says. But if we knew that only, it would lead us to utter despair. We need faith because it teaches us a complementary truth: that wretched as we are,

God's love can save us. Writes Pascal, "There is a God, of whom men are capable, and there is a corruption of nature which makes them unworthy. It is of equal importance for men to know each of these points, and it is equally dangerous for man to know God without knowing his own wretchedness, as for him to know his own wretchedness without knowing the Redeemer who can cure him. Knowing only one of these points leads either to the arrogance of the philosopher, who knows God but not his own condition; or to the despair of the atheist, who knows his own wretchedness but not his Redeemer."

This is typical of the style in which Pascal writes. It is always carving out a middle ground between extremes, and its arguments are often based on paradox. Pascal's arguments are not linear, proceeding from A to Z. Rather, they are centripetal, moving from the outside of the circle to its center. The center is the same, and it is God. His logic is discontinuous, in that it starts from different points, but all lines of argument converge at the same place. "Jesus Christ is the object of all things, the center toward which all things tend," Pascal writes. Thus, his book has a theological unity which transcends its literary topsy-turviness.

A paradox that strikes a reader throughout *Pensées* is that Pascal must constantly use reason in order to convince us that reason is ineffective in demonstrating spiritual truths. This undercuts his argument, because it is essentially a spiritual argument, and to the extent that Pascal makes it successfully, he vindicates reason's ability to make such arguments.

Pascal deals with this unintentional support he gives to reason by making large concessions to the anti-reason position, skepticism. He asks the scientists how they can be so confident that their experiences and experiments are all true. "No one can be sure, apart from faith, whether he is sleeping or walking, because when we are asleep we are just as firmly convinced that we are awake as we are now." Pascal raises the possibility that "the other half of our lives, when we think we are awake, is just another sleep slightly different from the first." His point is that often reason is dependent on certain assumptions taken for granted, which is another way of saying, taken on faith.

Pascal is not saying that we cannot distinguish between dreams and reality. His point is the opposite: of course we know when we are awake. How do we know? "Because we know" is probably the answer he would give. "Intuitively" is another way of putting it. We certainly don't know by some sort of ratiocinative process.

For Pascal there are fundamental truths and there are other truths. The fundamental truths, such as whether we exist and when we are awake, are discernible through faith. The heart is more important than the mind in such things. Supernatural matters are not accessible to the senses, because by definition, they run counter to the senses, nor are they accessible to the natural intellect, because by definition, they transcend it.

For example, Pascal notes that "without doubt nothing is more shocking to our reason than to say that the sin of the first man has implicated in its guilt men so far from the original sin that they seem incapable of sharing it." It is not much good to reply that the ancestors of Adam and Eve sin just as their first parents did, because had their first parents not sinned, the rest of us would be in an entirely different situation. Maybe we, too, would have eaten of the apple, but presumably with our free will from God we could also have refused it. Because of the sin of Adam and Eve, we never have that particular choice. Pascal's conviction is that you cannot rationally explain how original sin is inherited by all men — this lies outside the bounds of human intelligence; only the divine intelligence understands. And yet nothing is more important to the Christian faith than the fact that we are all born with original sin — even the crucifixion presupposes this.

Another limitation of reason that Pascal points out is that it does not govern the daily lives of most people, and it governs only a small fraction of the lives of intellectuals. Most of our activities, Pascal rightly notes, are based on habit, and most of our beliefs on faith. For example, when we hear on the news that the president is visiting Australia, we don't demand verification that the president exists (even though we haven't met him), that Australia exists (even though we haven't been there), and that the reporters aren't lying to us when they report on the trip. We take all this on faith, or more precisely, we take it on the authority of the press and the people who make maps. Pascal tells us that the mind is a sort of "automaton" which often acts not on proof but "the easier belief of habit." We cannot prove that the sun will rise tomorrow; we can only assume that it will, yet few of us lose sleep worrying that it will not. Pascal defends religious doctrines and standard prayers on the grounds that they don't have to be proved every day; rather, they become integrated in the lives of Christians, and are sustained by force of habit.

There is no concrete effort in *Pensées* to prove God's existence, but outlines of proofs are suggested. Pascal rejects Aquinas's proof that the order and beauty of creation presuppose a divine intelligence behind it; there is in the universe "too much order to deny and not enough to affirm" God's existence. In other words, there is the beauty of the rainbow, which points to God's design; but there is also the ugliness of the earthquake, which suggests some primordial chaos.

Pascal is impressed by the improbability of Catholicism: here is another paradoxical reason for his belief in it. "There is something astonishing about Christianity," he writes, "and it is not because I was born in it. Far from it; I stiffen myself against it for that very reason, for fear of being corrupted by prejudice. But though I was born in it, I cannot help finding it astonishing."

What's so astonishing about it? Everything, says Pascal. Take Christian doctrines: the fall of mankind, the resurrection of Jesus, and so on. These are very implausible notions to most people. It is easily understandable that a caveman would draw pictures of the sun on his wall, because that is what he sees. It is not easily understandable that highly educated men for several hundred years would place their deepest trust in the idea that an angel refused to obey his Creator, that this angel corrupted the first man and woman, that the Creator sent his Son as a man to die for mankind, and that this Son was taken into heaven after the job was done so he could reign in glory. The Christian religion has established itself throughout the world, and so gently and firmly, "even though it is so contrary to nature," Pascal says. This strongly suggests that its tenets must be true.

Another astonishing thing is creation — the fact that babies are born. What grounds does the atheist have, Pascal wants to know, for saying that Christ could not rise from the dead? "Which is harder, to be born or to rise again? That what has never been should be, or that what has been should be once more? Is it harder to come into existence or to come back?" Modern thinkers are scornful of the idea of miracles even though things they

101

take for granted are, in many ways, much more miraculous than changing water into wine, or walking on the water.

Pascal believes in miracles, and thinks they are central to the faith. In fact, this, he says, is what distinguishes Catholicism from other religions — our miracles work. What is the proof? Pascal takes the case against miracles and turns it on its head. "Instead of concluding that there are not true miracles because there are so many false ones, we must on the contrary say that there certainly are true miracles since there are so many false ones." This seems an odd sort of reasoning, but there is a logic to it. After all, Pascal asks, how could people place their faith in miracles if there were thousands of miracles alleged through history, and all of them were proved false? "There could not possibly be so many false miracles enjoying so much credit, unless some of them were genuine," Pascal says.

As an analogy, consider the used-car salesman. How could he possibly persuade anybody, let alone thousands of people, to buy his cars if all of them were lemons? Obviously, some of the cars are lemons, and this makes us suspicious when we buy; but if all were that way, he might as well go out of business. Yet used cars — and miracles — have been around for a very long time. Clearly there must be something to some of them.

In the midst of all these charming and intuitive arguments, Pascal throws in a very powerful scientific argument for the existence of God. This has become famous as Pascal's probability proof for God. Basically, Pascal argues that the risk of believing in God if he exists (metaphysical damnation) is far smaller than the risk of not believing in God if he does exist (eternal damnation). Either we can believe in God or we can reject him.

Either God exists or he does not. Pascal is saying that if we believe and are in fact wrong, then we lost little or nothing. But if we don't believe and are wrong, the consequences are dire. So every reasonable person should bet on the odds. This argument has never been refuted, but it does suffer from one limitation. It does not really prove God's existence. All it proves is that it makes sense to believe in God. Notice that the main thrust of the argument is that it makes sense to believe in God *even if God does not exist.*

Pascal then criticizes the philosophy of deism, popular in his time. Deism holds that God is the "watchmaker" who makes his clock and winds it up, but then does not interfere with it. This notion of God, as a creative impersonal force, Pascal found mystifying and revolting. Deism is "almost as remote from the Christian religion as atheism," he says. "The Christian God does not consist merely of a God who is author of mathematical truths and the order of the elements."

Rather, Catholicism "consists in the mystery of the Redeemer, who, uniting in himself the two natures, human and divine, saved men from the corruption of sin in order to reconcile them with God in his divine person." This notion of a personal God was central for Pascal. "It is not only impossible but useless to know God without Christ. Christ is the mediator without whom all communication with God is broken." Pascal does not understand how people can selectively use the Catholic faith. "How I have such foolishness as not believing in the Eucharist, etc. If the Gospel is true, if Jesus Christ is God, where is the difficulty?" The point is, if God exists, everything is possible, including miracles, floods, Jonah in the whale's belly, everything.

Pascal believed in his heart that there was no salvation outside the body of the Catholic Church. Thus, though he had certain reservations about it, he never departed from orthodoxy, and he believed even when it was contrary to his reason — indeed often because it was contrary to his reason. There are a few reformist passages in *Pensées*: at one point Pascal says, "It is an appalling thing that the discipline of the Church today is represented as so excellent that any attempt to change it is treated as a crime." Yet he calls for changes to be made "with circumspection."

He defends the authority and teaching of the Catholic Church. To his Jansenist friends who invoke Saint Augustine's writings on grace to challenge ecclesiastical authorities Pascal writes, "If Augustine were to appear today and enjoy as little authority as his modern defenders concede, he would not accomplish anything."

On the sacrament of confession, Pascal writes, "The Catholic religion does not oblige us to reveal our sins indiscriminately to everyone. It allows us to remain hidden from all other men, with one single exception, to whom it bids us reveal our innermost heart. It lays on this man the obligation of inviolable secrecy, which means that he may as well not possess the knowledge of us that he has. Can anything milder and more charitable be imagined? And yet, such is the corruption of man that he finds this law harsh, and this is one of the main reasons why a large part of Europe has revolted against the Church. How unjust and unreasonable the heart of man, that he should resent the obligation to behave toward one man and it would be right, in some ways, to behave toward all. For is it right that we should deceive them?"

Pascal is not able, in this outline of his meditations, to give us a clear picture of what the relation between Church and State should be, of what power the Church should have. But he does dispel many silly slogans. It is said, for example, that "might does not make right," and thus the Church, which is concerned with what is right, should be powerless. But Pascal points out that it is not a question of might versus right; we need both: "Right without might is helpless; might without right is tyrannical. Right without might is challenged, because there are always evil men about. Might without right is denounced. We must therefore combine might and right, and to that end make right into might or might into right."

These are the insights which we find in *Pensées*, a book which has inspired countless generations of French Catholics and people around the world. In a sense it is appropriate that the book should be sketchy and incomplete, because it is written with the aid of reason and we know by now Pascal's view of its limitations.

Through pressure from Catholic authorities and his Jansenist friends Pascal was, in the last years of his life, forced to choose between the two faiths — and he chose Catholicism. At the same time he continued his correspondence with the Jansenists at Port Royal. His last days were unfortunate ones, however. He suffered a succession of illnesses, now suspected to be tuberculosis and cancer, but the doctors who treated him were inept. They failed to diagnose his sickness and made prescriptions which exacerbated his sorry condition. He wanted to receive Extreme Unction (as the sacrament of the anointing of the sick used to be called), but the last rites were held from him because he was thought not to be fully aware of what he was asking for. Finally, his pleas were granted and he received the sacrament; a few days later he died, on August 19, 1662, happy to be reunited with his Maker. He was buried at St. Étienne du Mont.

S • E • V • E • N

thomas à kempis's

imitation of christ

THE *Imitation of Christ* is perhaps the best-loved work of Christian meditation ever published. It is not a text for intellectuals — in some ways, it is consciously anti-intellectual — and yet it contains truths and wisdom that often transcend the intellect. It speaks directly to the heart. Its message, briefly, is that we achieve joy on this earth and hereafter when we submit entirely to God. Our intellect and our emotions, both of which are vehicles to appreciate God and honor him, can also be obstacles to reaching him, Thomas reminds us. It is only when we resist their centrifugal tug, when we bring mind and heart into line with God, that we experience true happiness.

The *Imitation* is not, like the *Confessions* or the *Summa*, part of a historical literature that delineates the great events of the Catholic Church in Europe. Its origins are somewhat obscure, and the environment in which it was prepared quaint and secluded. The book was written by a monk for monks and its influence did not spread like a thunderbolt, but slowly, magically, as the love and beauty in the little text inspired individual persons and families and urged them to spread the message to others. Since the *Imitation's* first printing in 1472, several thousand editions and translations have appeared. Eventually even the intellectual community caught on, and the work has been garlanded in the most lavish terms by Charles Kingsley, Samuel Johnson, Thomas Carlyle, and countless others.

Although there is still some dispute over who actually wrote the *Imitation*, opinion has converged around the name of Thomas Haemerken, a monk from the hamlet of Kempen, a few miles north of present-day Düsseldorf. His life-story is an intriguing one. In 1392, at the age of only twelve, he walked from his hometown to the town of Deventer, in the Low Countries, where he joined the monastery supervised by Florent Radewijns, a successor to the great man who founded the monastery, Gerard Groote.

Ordained a priest in 1413 at the age of thirty-three, Thomas showed such evident spiritual gifts and devotion that he was elevated within the ranks of the monastery, first to treasurer, then to subprior. But spiritual blessing is not the same as administrative talent. Thomas served willingly but without distinction; his real interests and skills lay elsewhere: in recovering Catholic orthodoxy and spirituality in a difficult time for the Church.

Although removed from the center of theological controversy, the monastery was by no means immune from the deep currents of doubt that were coursing through the veins of the Church. Not only was medieval theology being openly contested, but the institutional Church was fragmented. Philip the Fair and Pope Boniface VIII were at odds, and Emperor Louis of Bavaria fought with three popes: John XXII, Benedict XII, and Clement VI. With Christians trying to distinguish Saint Peter's true successor among multiple popes and Catholic teaching under scrutiny, if not actual attack, on numerous fronts, how could even a rustic Low Country monastery be secure?

Fortunately in times of doubt and ruin, Catholicism has been known to raise great and noble souls who have stood athwart the decadence yelling "Stop!" Thomas à Kempis was such a soul. He was not planning on it: he came to Deventer to relish a life of work and peaceful prayer. The community he joined was called the Brothers of the Common Life; they came to be undistinguished. But soon Thomas found his mission to be a very high and urgent one indeed. It was to do nothing less than recover the embers of spiritual truth and experience of God that seem to have been smothered by abstract medieval theology. Being a monk who actually lived the common life, instead of a professor in a university, Thomas found himself able to communicate spiritual truths in a manner that people could not only understand but also feel.

This is one of the great virtues of the *Imitation*. It is not a theoretical document, for which it has been criticized, and yet that is its virtue. It is by no means the only work that Thomas produced. He has left behind a legacy of sermons, treatises on educating monks, devotional hymns, and biographies of Saint Lydwine and Gerard Groote. But the *Imitation* remains the most profound of his writings and retains its relevance to the current day.

In its candor and simplicity, it had a powerful impact on the way religious people wrote about their experiences with God. Previous writings tended to be Latinized and ornate, full of heavy and sometimes stretched metaphor, almost pompous in tone. Thomas showed that devotional writing was best done in simple language. God communicates with the heart in a straight line, after all, not via winding roads with bewildering signs and detours.

Since Thomas, many scholars and monks simplified their styles so that the English language benefited from a fresh and simple prose that said precisely what it meant.

The *Imitation* begins by taking into account the negative reverberations in the Catholic world. "It is often seen that those who hear the Gospels find little sweetness in them," notes Thomas. "The reason is that they do not have the spirit of Christ." If we wish to understand the Gospels, he says, "we must conform our life as nearly as we can to Christ." Here we have an echo of Saint Augustine's famous epithet, "Believe, and you will understand." Unfortunately most people want to do it the other way around.

Thomas is not against an intellectual approach per se, but he writes that "deeply inquisitive reasoning does not make a man holy or righteous, but a good life makes him beloved by God." Thomas seems to feel that intelligence, like other forms of riches, poses grave temptations for the soul. "The more knowledge you have, the more grievously will you be judged for its misuse, if you do not live according to it," he warns.

"He is most unwise who gives heed to any other thing except what will profit him to the health of his soul," Thomas says. "The highest and most profitable learning is this: that a man have a truthful knowledge and a full despising of himself." Here Thomas seems to be counseling self-abasement, and he is called to account for it. But in his time many churchmen and theologians were fattened with intellectual pride in their sophisticated arguments; all this is useless, Thomas says, unless it is put to God's service. He does not really want men to despise themselves, but he realizes that it is only when man knows how sinful and limited he is that he can find full joy and gratitude in his benevolent Creator.

"Well-ordered learning is not to be belittled, for it is good and comes from God," Thomas clarifies, "but a clean conscience and a virtuous life are much better and more to be desired." In reading the Bible, for example, "we ought to seek spiritual profit rather than elegance of style, and to read simple and devout books as gladly as books of high learning and wisdom."

Thomas is as wary of the emotions as of the intellect. "The eye is not satisfied or pleased with seeing any material thing, nor the ear with hearing. Those who follow their own sensuality hurt their own cause and lose the grace of God." He wins the grace of God, Thomas says, "who is little in his own right and who sets at naught all worldly honor and pleasure."

There is a great advantage to an approach which counts the intellect and the senses for little and simply follows and praises God in all things. First, it is easier to appreciate a divine plan at work, Thomas implies. When things go well, for instance, one praises God's munificence; when they go badly, one realizes that God is putting one to the test. This may strike the empiricist and the cynic as circular reasoning; in fact, it is not "reasoning" at all; it is simply God's truth. "The beginning of all evil temptations is inconstancy of mind and too little trust of God," writes Thomas.

Another advantage to Thomas's advice is that it strengthens the believer in times of adversity. Thomas puts it best: "When a good man is troubled or tempted, or disquieted by evil thoughts, then he understands and knows that God is most necessary to him, and that he may do nothing that is good without God. Then the good man sorrows and weeps and prays because of the miseries he rightly suffers. Then the wretchedness of this life burdens him too, and he yearns to be dissolved from this body of death and to be with Christ, for he sees that there can be no full peace or perfect security here in this world."

Thomas knows that men must indeed erect sturdy defenses against temptation, and they need God's grace to do this. Some may think Thomas demands too much. "When a man has true sorrow for his sins, all worldly comforts are painful to him." And further: "You should behave in every deed and in every thought as though you were about to die this very instant." Thomas seems not only to oppose all forms of pleasure, he even seems to oppose life itself. "Long life," he warns, "often brings only an increase in sin." Is this a man you want to invite to the picnic?

The reason for Thomas's stern warnings is that he knows how dangerous and crafty the devil is, how he manipulates people into sin, how fragile are human defenses against Lucifer, the fallen angel. Sometimes temptation is almost too strong to resist, Thomas knows; the only remedy, according to him, is preemption. "As medicine for the body is administered too late when the sickness has been allowed to increase by long continuance, so it is with temptation. First, an unclear thought comes to mind, then follows a strong phantasm, then pleasure in it and various evil motions, and at the end follows a full consent; so, little by little, the enemy gains full entrance, because he was not wisely resisted at the beginning. The slower a man is in resisting, the weaker he is to resist, and the enemy is daily stronger against him." Has there ever been a finer, a more accurate, account of how the devil's wiles work on the human heart?

The second reason for Thomas's warnings is that he knows how terrible it is to be condemned. Most of us do not spend much time thinking about damnation. Yet if there is heaven there is also hell: the concept of "saved" is meaningless unless placed alongside the concept of "damned." Thomas is eager that we not think of hell only when we are at the lips of the precipice, struck by some terrible illness or crippled with old age. Because then we might not have the opportunity to repent at the last moment, either because death comes suddenly, or because we are too weak of body or consciousness to be able to repent.

One sees in Thomas's view of hell a resemblance to Dante's circles of suffering, corresponding to various sins: "A man will be most punished in the things in which he most offended," writes Thomas. "Slothful persons will in purgatory be pricked with burning prongs of iron, and gluttons will be tormented with great hunger and thirst. Lecherous persons and lovers of voluptuous pleasure will be filled with burning pitch and brimstone, and envious persons will wail and howl as mad dogs. The proud man will be filled with shame and confusion, and the covetous man pinched with penury and need." Unlike those of us who feel occasional relief from our earthly travails, and get consolation from our friends, Thomas says the souls of the damned know no rest or commiseration. It is almost too horrible to contemplate.

So how is one to gain salvation in the face of this? First, Thomas seems to suggest, we should pay attention to our own weaknesses. "You will never be a spiritual man and a devout follower of Christ unless you can keep from meddling in other men's deeds and, especially, can give heed to your own deeds." Most people, unfortunately, behave as though they regard the Ten Commandments as admirably suited to the needs of their neighbors. Thomas urges them to be more spiritually introspective, to cast the plank from their own eyes before seeking to remove the mote from their neighbors' eyes.

Second, Thomas counsels good men and women to beware of praise. This principle — to be careful of anything that makes you feel wise or good — runs throughout the *Imitation*. The reason for the suspicion is that Thomas feels that when a person feels good about himself his defenses are lowered, and the devil has an easier time striking. "You are not better because you are praised, or the worse because you are blamed, for you are as you are, and whatever is said of you, you are not better than Almighty God." On one level this advice is obvious, yet apparently it is not obvious enough, because few people act in accordance with it.

We should be wary of praise of ourselves, but we should constantly praise and thank God, the genesis of our lives and everything that is good for us. "The greatest reason why the gifts of grace do not easily come to us is that we are ungrateful to the Giver, and render no thanks to him from whom all good things come. Grace is always given to those ready to give thanks for it."

With these thanks and this grace, says Thomas, comes not suffering but a joy that exceeds all earthly joys. Because this divine joy is so intense, earthly pleasures no longer seem to matter so much. The contempt which the Christian earlier forced himself to feel for temporal titillations is replaced by indifferences — the person who has experienced Christ simply has no urge to return to the evanescent corruptions of the flesh and the intellect. "Truly, if you had once entered the bloody wounds of Jesus, and had there tasted a little of his love, you would care nothing for the liking or the disliking of the world, but would rather have great joy when wrongs and injuries were done to you, or perfect love of God makes a man perfectly to disregard himself."

In order to become one with Christ we have to die unto ourselves — this goes back to the New Testament. It is remarkable how frank Thomas is concerning this, though. He boldly urges Christians to "inwardly lift up your mind to God, so that you regard outward things little." Is this good advice? Is Thomas asking us to abandon our earthly responsibilities? Actually, he is giving no more than the biblical command to be "in the world but not of it." Perhaps being a Christian absorbed in Christ's love will bring indifference to certain worldly pleasures, but this absence of mind merely denotes a presence of soul. Life is lifted onto a higher plane.

"It is not lawful to forsake all things, for physical nature must be preserved," Thomas allows, but he prays that God will grant him "grace to use bodily necessities temperately." Christians should make their "flesh subject to the will of the spirit, and chastise and compel it to serve, until it can learn to be content with a little and to delight in simple things, not murmuring or objecting because of any contrary thing that may befall it." There is a rationale for this from a purely earthly point of view as well: with lower expectations even moderate achievements make us happy; when we expect great things we are dissatisfied even with the good.

Reading all this the reader, perhaps, gets a sinking feeling and may ask the logical question: Am I capable of all this? "Jesus has many lovers of his kingdom, but he has few bearers of his cross," Thomas says. He makes the road to heaven seem difficult indeed. "If a man gives all his possessions for God, he yet is nothing, and if he does great penance for his sins, and if he has great wisdom and knowledge, he yet is far from virtue. And if he has great virtue and devotion, he yet lacks much, and there is especially one thing most necessary to him."

What? "That he go clearly out of himself and keep nothing to himself of any private love." There is no one richer and better off, says Thomas, than "he who can forsake himself and all passing things and truly hold himself to be the lowest and meanest of all in God's sight."

It is true that Thomas wrote for other monks, and one may read him thinking that his is far too difficult a regimen for ordinary people, even committed Catholics. But in fact Thomas is simply trying to strengthen our "spiritual armor," as he calls it. "Saints did not have special spiritual comfort," he reminds us. "They had many great griefs and various temptations and great desolation, but they bore all with patience and trusted more in God than in themselves." If the starting point is right — if we really trust God and his word above ourselves in all matters — then we will be able to meet the stern tasks ahead of us, Thomas implies.

An essential part of the Christian regimen, as Thomas outlines it, is the regular receiving of the sacraments, especially Holy Communion. Without this "heavenly meat," as he calls the wafer dipped in wine, we will surely perish, says Thomas. He acknowledges that the ritualistic consumption of the Sunday host may not be all that is needed for salvation and yet Thomas acknowledges, "If I am now often negligent and slothful, even when I have been to Communion, what would I be if I had not received that blessed medicine and not sought that great help?"

Thomas calls the Eucharist "God's holy institution, and not man's invention." He reveres the sacrament as well as the Mass which places Holy Communion at its center. "When a priest says Mass he honors God," writes Thomas. "He makes the angel glad. He edifies the Church. He helps the people who are living. He gives rest to those who are dead. And he makes himself partaker of all good deeds."

This, in brief, is the message of the *Imitation*. Because it is in some ways a difficult one, and because people are reluctant to face it, the book has been criticized on several grounds. One concern is that the book is too negative and instills gloom and foreboding in the reader, an attitude that may not be conducive to approaching the Christian mission with courage and confidence. A second criticism is that Thomas does not deal sufficiently in theological concepts — his spiritualistic prose might be misinterpreted by those unlearned in theology, so they may fall into all sorts of deviations and errors. A final point is that Thomas is far too severe on earthly knowledge and earthly pleasures — after all, why did God give us our intelligence and senses if not to use and appreciate them?

These are not criticisms totally devoid of merit. While it is true that the *Imitation* places difficult challenges before Christians and insists upon fear of God and deep compunction for offending him, it is always clear that the goal of this is spiritual emancipation, the spirit released from the burden of sin, man brought into the bliss that only God can give. So the road of thorns leads to the heavenly castle and, as Thomas makes very clear, there is a seat at the table for everybody. With such succulent fare waiting, Thomas's insistence that we constantly praise God and give thanks for our blessings does not seem a tall request.

The *Imitation* was never intended to be a theological treatise. It was written for monks in monasteries where orthodoxy is presumed. Lay people, too, should go elsewhere for their catalog of doctrines. The *Imitation* does not pretend to be the only book a Catholic should read, or a book that embraces every aspect of the Catholic faith. It is a small slice, perhaps, but it is a delicious and important morsel. It can be savored without wondering if it has all the ingredients and vitamins necessary to the full Catholic life.

It should not be thought that at any point in his life, or at any point in the *Imitation*, Thomas is unorthodox or deviates from Catholic teaching. Because he believed in submitting totally to God, and because he accepted that the Catholic Church was God's Church on earth, Thomas gladly submitted to all of its doctrines without question.

An incident in his life vividly illustrates this. In the year 1422, problems developed in the monastery when the four churches of the area elected Rudolph of Diepholt to succeed the late Frederick of Blankenhem to the episcopal see. When Pope Martin V heard about this and was informed that Rudolph was illiterate and even mentally incompetent, he replaced him with Seuder of Culenborg. But for some strange reason the leaders of the four churches insisted on having Rudolph. They wanted him badly enough to defy the pope, who placed the diocese under interdict — which meant that sacraments were withheld in most cases, and dissidents were barred from church services.

The citizens of the area then demanded that the clergy either administer sacraments or leave. The order to which Thomas belonged chose exile rather than disobedience to the pope, even though they lived there since their founding, and were fiercely attached to the pristine setting. Thomas, who was part of the leadership in the monastery that made the decision, moved to another monastery at Lunenkerk near Harlingen, where he lived out the last few years of his life.

The charge that the *Imitation* is anti-intellectual has perhaps the greatest merit of the accusations slung against the book. Indeed the phrase most often cited to back this up does tend to alarm people who value the mind highly: "I would rather feel compunction of heart for my sins," says Thomas, "than know the definition of compunction." To which an Aquinas might have protested, "Why not both?"

There are passages where Thomas seems to downplay intellectual comprehension too much. "Beware not to dispute high matters and the secrets of judgment," he warns in the *Imitation*. "Why this man is so abandoned and forsaken by God, why this man is given so great grace, why one man is so much troubled and another is so greatly advanced — these things surpass all man's knowledge that no man's reason or inquisition can suffice to search God's judgments."

Perhaps Thomas is right that ultimately a lot of these questions dissolve into mystery. But surely it cannot be wrong to apply the mind that God gave man to questions that bear on his condition not just in the next world but also in this one. At certain points in the *Imitation* Thomas sounds like he agrees. Perhaps the explanation, then, is this: Thomas believes that the intellect is so often misused that he wishes his book to be a warning against intellectual pride and excess. Certainly he is right that, in the final count, it is the spirit that is more important, for through the spirit comes the redeeming grace of God, who is spirit himself.

Thomas à Kempis died on July 25, 1471, having completed, says the Chronicle of Mount Agnes, "on the feast of Saint James the Greater, the 92nd year of his age, the 63rd of his religious life, and the 58th of his priesthood."

newman's

apologia pro vita sua

J OHN Henry Newman tells us: "It is better for the sun and moon to drop from heaven, for the earth to fall, and for all the many millions on it to die of starvation in extremest agony, as far as temporal affliction goes, than that one soul, I will not say, should be lost, but should commit one single venial sin, should tell one willful untruth, or should steal one poor farthing without excuse."

More than any single person, John Henry Newman is responsible for legitimizing Catholicism in Britain. Before the publication of his classic, *Apologia Pro Vita Sua* (an account of his religious conversion and beliefs), it was still fashionable to espouse anti-Catholic and anti-papist sentiments in England. Certainly prejudice against Catholics was not entirely obliterated after Newman's book, but it was severely truncated, rendered crass and objectionable in polite company. Reading the *Apologia*, one sees how a single text could have such an impact. It is a powerful and moving account of an Anglican priest's conversion to the Catholic Church, and his painful attempt to justify this shift to the very community he has left.

Newman did not simply sit down, on some divine afflatus, to write the *Apologia*. It was provoked by a series of attacks on his character and indeed on all Catholics by Charles Kingsley, prominent Anglican chaplain, professor at Cambridge University, author of *Westward Ho!* "Truth, for its own sake, had never been a virtue with the Roman clergy," Kingsley wrote in *Macmillan's Magazine* in December 1863. "Father Newman informs us that it need not, and on the whole, ought not to be; that cunning is the weapon which heaven has given to the saints wherewith to withstand the brute male force of the wicked world which marries and is given in marriage. Whether his notion be doctrinally correct or not, it is at least historically so."

When Newman protested "this grave and gratuitous slander" to *Macmillan's* he received a reply from Kingsley offering to withdraw the charge based on Newman's assurance that he did not mean it. But Newman was not satisfied, as his ironic rebuttal in the form of a dialogue indicates:

> I rejoin: *Mean* it! I maintain I never *said* it, whether as a Protestant or as a Catholic.
>
> Mr. Kingsley replies: I waive that point.
>
> I object: Is it possible? What? Waive the main question! I either said it or I didn't. You have made a monstrous charge against me, direct, distinct, public. You are bound to prove it as directly, as distinctly, as publicly — or to own you can't.
>
> Well, says Mr. Kingsley, if you are quite sure you did not say it, I'll take your word for it; I really will.
>
> My *word*? I am dumb. Somehow I thought that it was my *word* that happened to be on trial. The word of a Professor of Lying, that he does not lie.

By the time of the publication of Newman's call for vindication in the form of a pamphlet, the controversy had become one of the spiciest on the European continent. Unfortunately for Kingsley, but fortunately for Catholicism, the Anglican teacher and writer was not sufficiently chastised. He wrote a booklet full of the most acrimonious attacks on Newman personally and the Catholic Church generally. It was titled "What, Then, Does Dr. Newman Mean?" To this crude and virulent document, Newman's *Apologia* was a fitting reply.

The *Apologia* would be of passing interest if it was merely a clever riposte in a nineteenth-century dispute. But it is far more than that. By enlarging the scope of the debate, by reading Kingsley's booklet to be a call for Newman to justify his presence in the Catholic Church, Newman elevated a newspaper grudge into a monumental defense of Catholic orthodoxy over Protestant liberalism. In the process he achieved far more than the vindication of one man who had incurred the suspicion of British elites for defecting from the Anglican faith; somehow Newman spoke, in one voice, for an entire generation of Catholics in England, who felt cornered and uncomfortable practicing what was derisively termed "Romanism," who wanted to be able to worship on their own terms, who needed to communicate to their Anglican friends what it really meant to be a Catholic.

Newman was aware that he was starting out the *Apologia* as an underdog. After all, his main audience was the very Anglican community with which he had broken when he became a Catholic priest. "I must break through this barrier of prejudice against me if I can, and I think I shall be able to do so," he writes. He is referring not only to a general antipathy toward Catholicism but also a particular suspicion toward him, especially intense at Newman's alma mater, Oxford. Even while he was an Anglican, Newman had been critical of Protestantism, and his famous *Tract 90* had drawn fire from a body of European bishops. To some Anglican scholars and prelates, Newman had spent years in the Anglican Church as a closet Catholic, receiving orders from Rome, and quitting Anglicanism at the strategic moment calculated to give it maximum embarrassment and bring maximum rewards to the Vatican.

It is not easy to overcome feelings like this against you, thus Newman starts his *Apologia* with an account of the beginning of his life. He was born John Henry Newman to middle-class parents on February 21, 1801 in London. He attended a private school at Ealing where, he reports, "by the time I was fifteen my masters had nothing to teach me." At age fifteen he came to Trinity College, Oxford, where he would spend the next twenty-nine years, studying and teaching.

At first Trinity made a terrible impression. "I really think," Newman writes elsewhere, "if anyone should ask me what qualifications were necessary to Trinity, I would say there was only one: drink, drink, drink." But his revulsion for this turned him toward his books, and he spent, on average, six hours a day reading. In 1818 Newman was elected Scholar of Trinity.

Newman soon came under the influence of some brilliant and distinguished writers and teachers who were to have a profound influence on him, and later he on them. From William Hawkins, provost at Oriel College at Oxford, Newman learned about the value of religious tradition. Hawkins was an orthodox Anglican, yet he understood that contrary to what a lot of Protestants said, not all religious truths are contained in Scripture. "The sacred text was never intended to *teach* doctrine," Newman writes, "but only to *prove* it, and if we would learn doctrine, we must have recourse to the formularies of the church, for instance the catechism. . . . After learning from them the doctrines, the inquirer must *verify* them by Scripture."

Another colleague of Newman's was the erratic iconoclast Hurrell Froude, a fellow at Oriel. "He professed openly his admiration of the Church of Rome, and his hatred of the Reformers. He delighted in the notion of a hierarchical system, of sacerdotal power, and of full ecclesiastical liberty. . . . He had a high severe idea of the intrinsic excellence of virginity, and he considered the Blessed Virgin its great pattern. He delighted in thinking of the saints; he had a vivid appreciation of the idea of sanctity. . . . He had a deep devotion to the Real Presence [in the sacrament]. He was powerfully drawn to the medieval church." Newman comments that Froude's opinions "arrested and influenced me, even when they did not gain my assent." What Froude did teach Newman was "to look with admiration toward the Church of Rome, and in the same degree to dislike the Reformation," also to develop "an idea of devotion to the Blessed Virgin."

For all this, Newman was a firm Anglican. Although Anglicans are Protestants it must be remembered that they became so because of a quirk of history — the event centering on King Henry VIII and his passion for a second wife that the pope would not approve. It was lust, and not doctrinal difference, which brought about the Anglican separation from Rome. Later the Anglican Church took on some of the slogans of Protestantism, but in many respects it remained theologically and ritually close to the Catholic Church. Newman could believe in the Real Presence of God in the Eucharist and in reverence for the Virgin Mary without violating the canons of Anglicanism.

What sharply separated Newman from the Catholic Church — and this should come as no surprise — is that Newman believed from his youth that "the pope is the Antichrist." In fact, at Christmas in 1824 he preached a sermon to that effect. Newman says he followed distinguished Protestant authorities in believing that Gregory I, around the year 600, was the first pope who sold out to the devil, and the Council of Trent in the sixteenth century cemented the Catholic alliance with Mephistopheles. Further, Newman felt Catholics practiced idolatry in their worship of the Virgin Mary and the saints; oddly, his increasing admiration for the Mother of God and the martyrs did nothing to dilute Newman's objections on this point, because, he writes, he felt "these glorified creations of God would be gravely shocked, if pain could be theirs, at the undue veneration of which they were the objects."

In 1824 Newman took holy orders and was appointed curate of St. Clement's Church at Oxford. There he argued with the gloomy predestinarians, who said that man is totally corrupt; Newman's view was that men "are not so good as they should be, and better than they might be." He rejected the Calvinist tradition in Protestantism which denies free will and makes a chasm not only between good and evil but also between the chosen few and the damned — even in this life. Newman preferred the Catholic view that "shades and softens the awful antagonism between good and evil, by holding that there are different degrees of justification, and that there is a great difference in point of gravity between sin and sin, that there is no certain knowledge given to any one that he is simply in a state of grace." Distinctions between sins and the perennial opportunity for repentance — these were what characterized Catholicism, and to these Newman was quite sympathetic.

During much of his Anglican years Newman devoted his energies to opposing theological liberalism, which was becoming very fashionable in his time, and which he felt was making a "shipwreck of the faith." Why? Because Newman considered religious liberalism to be a policy of appeasement. Whenever it came into conflict with modernism — modern thought as represented by astronomy, Darwin, German transcendentalism — it yielded on all essential points. Liberals considered this the best way to preserve Christianity in a changing world, but to Newman it was a formula for surrender, an acknowledgment that the Christians were wrong and the secularists were right. Newman saw, moreover, that religious liberals were finding their own beliefs gradually eroded, until many of them were reduced to a religion of sentiment — they believed that most of the Bible was metaphor, that God was merely an extension of the laws of nature, and that as long as we are nice to our neighbors we are fulfilling God's plan for us.

Newman in the *Apologia* describes theological liberalism as "of a dry and repulsive character, not very dangerous in itself, though dangerous as opening the door to evils which it did not itself anticipate or comprehend." By admitting that Scripture was not inerrant, for example, liberalism left all the miracles and miraculous doctrines, including those central to Christianity such as the Resurrection, open to doubt. Newman proved prophetic in this concern; in our own day liberal clergy often deny such fundamental tenets of Christianity as Christ's bodily death, resurrection, and ascension into heaven.

The reason for liberalism's failure, Newman believed, was that it constituted "false liberty of thought, or the exercise of thought upon matters in which, from the constitution of the human mind, thought cannot be brought to any successful issue, and therefore is out of place. Among such matters are first principles of any kind, of these the most sacred and momentous are especially to be reckoned the truths of Revelation. Liberalism then is the mistake of subjecting to human judgment those revealed doctrines which are in their nature beyond and independent of it." Essentially, then, liberalism stemmed from pride. It was a case of the human mind trying to apprehend truths that were outside the orbit of reason, truths that could only be taken on faith.

From the speed with which liberalism was gaining favor among the clergy and intellectuals in England, Newman saw that it would need robust forces allied against it in order to cripple its proselytizing power. The problem for Newman was: How to resist this program to modify and erode the "great dogmas of the faith" that went by the name of liberalism? Would an orthodox Anglicanism and Protestantism be sufficient to oust so formidable an adversary? Ultimately Newman concluded that Catholicism was all that stood between liberalism and total victory; that, more than any other single factor, explains his astonishing decision to break with his church and join the Roman one.

But throughout the 1830s Newman resisted this solution, and developed instead his well-known *Via Media* ("middle course"), a sort of interregnum between Catholicism and Anglicanism, which he regarded as the strongest theological armor to withstand the liberal threat. Along with John Keble and Hurrell Froude, Newman founded the enormously influential Tractarian movement, which published regular tracts essentially affirming this centrist theological course which embraced Anglicanism but was, more precisely, equidistant from both the Church of England and the Church of Rome.

Newman's basic argument during this point in his life was that both Catholics and Anglicans descended from the same authentic religious roots — the "primitive" Church of Saint Augustine and Saint Athanasius. But both had departed from the original wisdom, Newman felt: the Catholic Church by "adding on" doctrines such as the Assumption of Mary into heaven; the Anglican Church for having cut itself off from the true Church through schism. "Each disputant has a strong point," Newman writes in the *Apologia*. "Our strong point is the argument from primitiveness, that of Romanists from universality." It is fact, Newman noted to the discomfort of many Anglican friends, "that we are estranged from the great body of Christians over the world."

The issue for Newman, then, was Catholicity versus Apostolicity. The ideal religion would embody both, would be universal and yet legitimately descended. Unfortunately Newman found himself in a world where one religion, the Catholic, had a claim to universality, and another, the Anglican, claimed it was truer to the teachings of the early Church. Newman's *Via Media*, then, was to nudge both "errant" theologies in the direction of what he considered the true Church, one which abjured the "errors" of both Catholicism and Anglicanism while retaining their good points.

Newman cites the three fundamental defining points of the *Via Media*: dogma, the sacramental system, and anti-Romanism. Unfortunately for him, many Anglicans found the third plank to be a bit of a sham. They did not think Newman's criticism of Rome was firm or strident enough. They saw him in the company of others like Froude who were openly affectionate toward the pope. They read Newman's students who went further than he did in vaunting Roman teaching. The renowned Edward Pusey and others at Oxford scolded Newman for being too "high church," but as the years went on, Newman was to ascend higher and higher until, in 1845, he would take Communion in his house at Littlemore and become a Catholic.

What caused Newman to bear out the dire predictions of his critics and move headlong toward Catholicism? Why did Newman leave what he himself termed "the happiest time of my life" in order to join a controversial group of papists? The first reason was a realization of a fundamental problem at the core of Protestantism. Protestants say they trust only in the word of the Bible, but nowhere does the Bible ask them to do this. It is Church tradition that has from the outset directed believers to Scripture as the inerrant word of God. Further, Newman saw that "every theology has its difficulties: Protestants hold justification by faith only, although there is no text in Saint Paul which enunciates it, and although Saint James explicitly denies it." He gives other examples.

Newman's study of two ancient Church controversies, the heresies of the Monophysites and the Arians, brought him something of an epiphany about Anglicanism. "It was difficult to make out how the Eutychians or Monophysites were heretics, unless Protestants and Anglicans were heretics also," Newman found. "It was difficult to [find arguments to] condemn the popes of the sixteenth century, without condemning the popes of the fifth." This was because "the principles and proceedings of the Church now, were those of the

Church then; the principles and proceedings of heretics then, were those of Protestants now."

This was confirmed in Newman's Arian study. He saw that the arguments of the reviled heretics were identical in substance, and very nearly in form, to those of his current-day Protestant friends, except that they tried to distinguish themselves from the early-Church heresies and claim a legitimate lineage back to Christ and the apostles. Newman discovered that this Protestant family tree had been faked; the Catholic Church, for all its institutional failings, had maintained spiritual continuity with its origins. "I found it so," Newman writes, "almost fearfully." As a result, his doctrine of the *Via Media* was, he admits, "in ruins."

Previously Newman had regarded the choice between the Catholic and Anglican churches as one between universality and antiquity. But his study of Saint Augustine, then as now a beacon that all Protestants cherish because of his emphasis on justification by faith, convinced Newman how wrong he had been. Saint Augustine was one of the prime oracles of antiquity, and yet Newman read of his reverence for the popes, his apparent conviction that one could not be saved outside the Roman Catholic Church, and the passion with which he fought those who tried to revise the teachings of the Church and polarize it. Newman wrote to a friend that this discovery was "the first real hit from Romanism" which he had felt, and that it gave him "a stomach ache."

From the end of 1841, Newman's *Apologia* tells us, "I was on my deathbed as regards my membership with the Anglican Church." He did not leave for four more years. But in 1842 Newman resigned his tutorship and chaplaincy at St. Mary's and moved to a retirement center at Littlemore. The reason was plain. Newman was not ready to become a Catholic yet, but he did not feel comfortable preaching in an Anglican church.

Shortly after his *Tract 90*, which defended certain Roman doctrines, Newman got a letter from a stranger who complained that Newman was converting his friends to Catholicism and would he be "good enough" to convert them back to Anglicanism? Newman, pained, replied, "Whatever be the influence of the Tracts, great or small, they may become just as powerful for Rome, if our Church refuses them, as they would be for our Church if she accepted them." But ultimately this answer proved unsatisfactory. As Newman confessed in a letter to John Keble, "I fear I must allow that, whether I will or no, I am disposing [my pupils] to Rome." This disturbed Newman because he himself had not taken the step of converting, so he didn't feel right in urging others upon a path that he himself was holding back from.

Controversy pursued Newman even to Littlemore. It bothered him, he acknowledges in the *Apologia*. "They persisted, what was I doing at Littlemore? Doing there! Have I not retreated from you? Have I not given up my position and my place? Am I alone, of Englishmen, not to have the privilege to go where I will, no questions asked?" Newman spent three years at Littlemore, shying away from seeing people, living a monastic and contemplative life in the company of a few of his most devoted pupils.

Gradually, Newman writes, "I came to see that the Anglican Church was formally in the wrong, and that the Church of Rome was formally in the right; so no valid reason could be assigned for continuing in the Anglican, and no valid objections could be taken to joining the Roman." In 1843 Newman published a retraction of his previous anti-Catholic statements. He says in the *Apologia* that "these words have been and are again and again cited against me, as if a confession that, when in the Anglican Church, I said things against Rome which I did not really believe." But Newman believed them at the time, he says, and the only reason his retraction was so strongly worded was because his original prejudices were stridently articulated, and Newman felt angry at the Anglican divines from whom he had absorbed this anti-Catholic bigotry.

Still, one doubt persisted in Newman's mind. For years he had defended what he calls "the dogmatic principle," or the principle of absolute truth, through the *Via Media*, and many had listened. "It is not easy, humanly speaking, to wind up an Englishman to a dogmatic level," Newman admits, and thus to persuade so many that the *Via Media* was preferable to theological liberalism was quite an accomplishment. But "in breaking the *Via Media* to pieces," Newman wondered, "would not dogmatic faith altogether be broken up?" In other words, was Newman striking an accidental blow for liberalism? "Oh, how unhappy this made me," Newman confesses.

It was only in 1845 that Newman realized that "either the Catholic religion is verily and indeed the coming of the unseen world into this, or there is nothing positive, nothing dogmatic, nothing real in any of our notions as to where we come or whither we go. There is no help for us: we must either give up the belief in the Church as a divine institution altogether, or we must recognize it in that communion of which the pope is the head. We must take things as they are: to believe in a church is to believe in the pope." Only Catholicism and not the "halfway house" of Anglicanism could defend against the rising tide of liberalism and secularism, Newman concluded.

On October 9, 1845 Newman was received into the Catholic Church by Father Dominic Barberi, a missionary priest from Italy. Newman felt relief for his soul, and yet there was a sadness. "How much I am giving up in so many ways. To me these are sacrifices irreparable, not only from my age, when people hate changing, but from my especial love of old associations and the pleasures of memory." Newman left Oxford in 1846, and was not to revisit it for at least thirty years. He paid one of the highest prices a man can pay for his convictions — the loss of a lifelong sense of place in life, estrangement from personal and intellectual companions who meant so much to him.

The next year Newman went to Rome and was ordained a Catholic priest. He was to rise rapidly through the ranks of the Catholic Church, despite opposition from some medieval-minded clergy such as Henry Manning, archbishop of Westminster, who still doubted Newman's orthodoxy. When Newman was made a cardinal he felt a final sense of vindication. "A cloud has been lifted from me forever," he exulted. He had justified himself, at last, to both Protestants and Catholics, and his integrity was intact.

The last part of the *Apologia* is a series of reflections on various aspects of Catholic orthodoxy. It also returns to several of Charles Kingsley's specific accusations against Newman, which are ably rebutted.

Newman starts out by telling his English readers, "I have changed in many things: in this I have not. From the age of fifteen, dogma has been the fundamental principle of my religion. I know no other religion. I cannot enter into the idea of any other sort of religion. Religion, as mere sentiment, is to me a dream and a mockery. As well can there be filial love without a father, as devotion without the fact of a Supreme Being."

After he became a Catholic Newman saw that his earlier concerns about "added on" Catholic doctrines were mistaken. Newman saw that there was a "principle of development" within the Church which "not only accounted for certain facts, but was in itself a remarkable philosophical phenomenon, giving a character to the whole course of Christian thought." In Catholicism there was a harmony, a continuity, and an individuality that no other religion had.

When Newman got to reading such Catholic saints as Alfonso Liguori, whom Kingsley had traduced, he found that there was none of the "Mariolatry" and contempt for Scripture that he had been told was contained in such books. Similarly in the *Exercises* of Saint Ignatius, Newman found "no cloud interposed between the creature and the object of his faith and love," that is, God. Protestants often complain that prayers to Mary and the saints interrupt the communication between man and God.

Newman says that upon becoming a Catholic, he had no difficulty accepting additional articles of faith that Catholics hold but Anglicans don't. Of course there were doubts and difficulties along the way, Newman writes, but "I have never been able to see a connection between apprehending those difficulties, and on the other hand doubting the doctrines to which they are attached. . . . A man may be annoyed that he cannot work out a mathematical problem, of which the answer is not given to him, without doubting that it admits of an answer, or that a certain particular answer is the true one."

Newman acknowledges that his original belief in God

is a gift not of intellectual apprehension but of faith. "If I looked into a mirror and did not see my face, I should have the sort of feeling which actually comes upon me, when I look into this living busy world, and see no reflection of its Creator. Were it not for this voice, speaking so clearly in my conscience and my heart, I should be an atheist."

Listing a catalog of the evils of the world, "the disappointments of life, the defeat of good, the success of evil, physical pain, mental anguish, the prevalence and intensity of sin, the pervading idolatries, and corruptions, the condition of the whole race," Newman speculates, "*since* there is a God, the human race is implicated in some terrible aboriginal calamity. It is out of joint with the purposes of its Creator. This is a fact, as true as the fact of existence. Thus the doctrine of what is theologically called original sin becomes to me almost as certain as that the world exists."

What about such a Catholic doctrine as the infallibility of the pope, which causes Protestants so much discomfort? "Supposing," writes Newman, "it is the will of the Creator to interfere in human affairs, and to make provisions for retaining in the world a knowledge of himself, so definite and distinct as to be proof against the energy of human skepticism; in such a case, there is nothing to surprise my mind, if he should think fit to introduce a power into the world, invested with the prerogative of infallibility in religious matters. Such a provision would be a direct, immediate, active, and prompt means of withstanding the difficulty; it would be an instrument suited to the need; and when I find that this is the very claim of the Catholic Church, not only do I feel no difficulty in admitting the idea, but there is a fitness in it, which recommends it to my mind." After all, says Newman, "experience proves that the Bible does not answer a purpose for which it was never intended." It may help with conversion, but a book "cannot make a stand against the wild living intellect of man" who wants to deviate from the truth.

Newman is, of course, not sympathetic to attacks on the Bible which seek to discredit it as the word of God. He detects "in many men of science or literature an animosity arising from almost a personal feeling; it being a matter of party, a point of honor, the excitement of a game, or a satisfaction to the soreness or annoyance occasioned by the acrimony or narrowness of apologists for religion, to prove that Christianity or that Scripture is untrustworthy." Writing at a time of burgeoning scientific developments threatening certain aspects of the faith, Newman is confident that there is no contradiction; but if there seems to be, he contends, the error is more likely with science. Scientific knowledge is always changing, Newman observes, so it is silly to follow the examples of religious liberals and modify eternal doctrines to suit the prevailing hypothesis in physics, chemistry, or astronomy.

Finally Newman settles on Kingsley's accusation of lying. This charge has long been defeated by the credibility with which Newman narrates the history of his religious views in the *Apologia*. Still, Newman faces the slander in all its specificity. He acknowledges that certain Catholic teachers have written that it can be moral to tell untruths under certain exceptional circumstances — say when telling an untruth will prevent the death of an innocent person — but so, Newman shows, did great Anglican divines, not to mention Milton, Paley, and Samuel Johnson. To permit equivocation in special or extreme cases is not to sanction routine falsehoods,

Newman says to his English audience. "You would have no fear of a man who you knew had shot a burglar dead in his own house, because you know you are not a burglar; so you would not think that Paley had a habit of telling lies in society, because in the case of a cruel alternative he thought it the lesser evil to tell a lie."

Newman closed his *Apologia* on this note. The reader, on shutting the book, feels a profound sense of admiration for this man's spiritual power, for his inspired intellect, for his courage and candor. Here is a book intensely personal in tone, dramatic despite its subject matter, vivid in its images, rising and falling in its modulations like the tides, held together with firm logical scaffolding.

Even though Newman's book greatly damaged Kingsley's reputation, Newman bore him no personal animosity. In the first pages of the *Apologia* he had said that this was no personal quarrel with Kingsley. "I am in warfare with him, but I wish him no ill. It is very difficult to get up resentment toward persons whom one has never seen." Rather, Newman was writing on behalf of the faith. And even though Kingsley never forgave Newman nor admitted his errors, when news of Kingsley's death reached Newman he grieved, and offered Mass for his soul.

Newman himself breathed his last on August 11, 1890, at the age of eighty-nine. Archbishop Manning, in a revised opinion, said of Newman's death, "We have lost our greatest witness for the faith." But in the *Apologia Pro Vita Sua*, perhaps the greatest "confession" since that of Saint Augustine, Cardinal Newman lives on, and Catholicism is stronger for that fact.

chesterton's

orthodoxy

W E are told that when G.K. Chesterton converted to Catholicism, the bishops in England celebrated by opening bottles of champagne. For decades Chesterton had been brilliantly agitating for Christianity. Nine years before his conversion he had written *Orthodoxy*, which was a Catholic apologia even though Chesterton didn't know it. (He was still an Anglican.) But ultimately Chesterton followed his writings to their logical conclusion. He entered the ranks of the Catholic Church, and took his seat at the table where the host was none other than Christ himself.

Born on May 29, 1874 in Kensington, a suburb of London, Chesterton was raised in the Unitarian faith by parents who were theologically and politically liberal. He found his Church's answers to the questions of the world inadequate, however, and by the time he entered St. Paul's School he was an agnostic. From his early years Chesterton developed an interest in writing and debating, and when he graduated from school he took up free-lance journalism.

In 1901 Chesterton married Frances Blogg. The couple moved to Battersea, where Chesterton began to write voluminously. He wrote a spate of novels, literary studies of Robert Browning and Charles Dickens, a famous set of detective stories called the Father Brown series, a play written at the urging of Chesterton's friend and debating partner George Bernard Shaw, even some heroic verse and ballad.

Heretics and *Orthodoxy*, Chesterton's two most famous works, were published in 1905 and 1908. By now Chesterton was clearly discomforted with agnosticism and had moved into a more mature Christianity than the ecclesiastical tidbits on which he had been raised. His Christian beliefs were crystallized in powerful intellectual opposition to leading liberal thinkers of Chesterton's day: George Bernard Shaw, H.G. Wells, Ibsen, and others.

Chesterton was, in life, an enormous man who weighed about three hundred fifty pounds. He loved to eat and drink almost as much as he loved to read and to argue. His prose had much of the zesty flavor of a couple of dozen pancakes eaten at breakfast. Fortunately it can be said of Chesterton that nothing he ever wrote was purely intellectual. Wherever his mind went, his ample body followed. *Orthodoxy*, like other Chesterton writings, reveals a man who has plunged heart, soul — and yes, stomach — into his work.

Orthodoxy is basically a book about romance, the romance of Christian orthodoxy. Chesterton's arguments are so surprising, his prose so clear and fresh, that reading the book for the first time is like riding a roller coaster for the first time as a youngster: all traditional categories are delightfully turned around; the world is made topsy-turvy, and the reader loves it.

Chesterton begins by setting before himself the task of defending his Christian beliefs. "I will not call it my philosophy," he says, "for I did not make it. God and humanity made it, and it made me." Immediately this most personal of texts moves from the subjective into the objective. Chesterton is not merely telling us what he feels, what his perspective happens to be. He is defining the nature of feeling itself, which is part of the nature of man.

Orthodoxy is no sterile text about natural law, however. It is rooted in common experience. Chesterton appeals directly to what people want for themselves in this life. He assumes that people want life to be a mixture of familiar things which can be regularly enjoyed and appreciated, like a good breakfast, and unfamiliar experiences which bring flavor and spice to the routine, like sunshine in the midst of the monsoon season. "I wish to set forth my faith as particularly answering this double need" for the tried and the unexpected, Chesterton writes.

He tells us where all this is going to lead — back to the center. Chesterton confesses that he has traversed all the long and winding roads of heterodoxy, the complex and alluring philosophies of his day. From naturalism to materialism to skepticism, these were all hailed as progressive. And "I did, like all other solemn little boys, try to be in advance of the age," says Chesterton. "Like them I tried to be ten minutes in advance of the truth. And I found that I was eighteen hundred years behind it." Chesterton said he leapfrogged from heresy to heresy, refining his world view all along. "And when I had put the last touches to it, I discovered that it was orthodoxy." This is an experience the French existentialist Albert Camus termed "revolt into orthodoxy." Chesterton was raised Christian and rebelled. Then he rebelled against that rebellion.

But his journey back to the faith is such a self-conscious and illuminating one that one is almost glad he had to leave the faith to come back. In the process, he familiarized himself intimately with the great lies and hoaxes of our times. The first of them is that all religions are basically the same and lead equally to God. Chesterton argues that Christianity is radically different. Unlike all other religions it seeks salvation not from within man but from the outside — from Christ. Other religions form a circle around man, a circle of law which if followed promises man virtue; but Christianity offers man something totally different — the cross.

Other religions are centripetal, says Chesterton, but Christianity is centrifugal: it breaks out. "For the circle is perfect and infinite in its nature, but it is fixed for ever in size, it can never be larger or smaller. But the cross, though it has at its heart a collision and a contradiction, can extend its four arms for ever without altering its shape. Because it has a paradox in its center it can grow without changing. The circle returns upon itself and is bound. The cross opens its arms to the four winds. It is a signpost for free travelers."

This is writing of a very high order which synthesizes metaphor and paradox with spiritual truth itself. Chesterton's writing is vivid with images from ritual and everyday life. Through these images he conveys truths that cannot otherwise be imagined. His own writing is riddled with paradoxes, but they do not confuse. They illuminate. And as Chesterton sees Christianity itself as fundamentally a paradox, a contradiction represented by the cross, his style is entirely appropriate to his subject.

One of the heresies that Chesterton sampled in early life was skepticism. Confronted with so many different answers to the nature of man, he was seduced into the explanation of the skeptic that all is for nought, that arguments proving this or that grand position were ultimately games and dodges, that even the senses were to be distrusted because observations were like mirages. Some philosophers had even raised the question of whether they (and mankind) existed, and severely chastised the medieval thinkers for taking such controversial things for granted. Hume and Descartes and the rest: they were such a fashionable and provocative lot.

Until Chesterton stopped to think: many of these ideas, when stretched to their extreme, resulted in peculiar and very damaging conclusions. Skepticism, in particular, was nothing else than a way for "the human intellect to destroy itself." Why? Because, says Chesterton, the skeptic must sooner or later ask himself, "Why should anything go right, even observation and deduction?" And if this is so, why should the skeptic be so confident in his reasoning that skepticism is the right philosophy? "The young skeptic says: I have a right to think for myself," comments Chesterton. "But the old skeptic, the completed skeptic, says: I have no right to think at all." Then knowledge itself is destroyed and man is restored to barbarism.

"There is the thought that stops thought," Chesterton realizes. "That is the only thought that ought to be stopped. That is the ultimate evil against which all religious authority was aimed." Here is a strange notion: religion developed as a means to conserve intellectual liberty and integrity. Usually religion is derided as an obstacle to free inquiry. But it is to protect it that "all the military systems in religion were originally ranked and ruled," writes Chesterton. "The creeds and the crusades, the hierarchies and the horrible persecutions were not organized, as is said, for the suppression of reason. They were organized for the difficult defense of reason. Man, by a blind instinct, knew that if once things were widely questioned, reason could be questioned first."

Here Chesterton is making the subtle point that both reason and revealed religion are ways of seeing the world, ways of accounting for man's experience. What few people realize is that neither system can be proved. There is a consistency within both frameworks, but neither can be justified from without. "They are both methods of proof which cannot themselves be proved," Chesterton notes. "In the act of destroying divine authority we have largely destroyed the idea of human authority" as well.

How is this so? Chesterton turns his attention to the mystery of causation which, he says, the scientists claim to have solved but are in utter ignorance about. Scientists begin with raw data which they take for granted for reasons that Chesterton cannot fathom. "They talk as if the fact that trees bear fruit were just as necessary as the fact that two and one trees make three." But that is not so because, as he puts it, "You cannot imagine two and one not making three, but you can easily imagine trees not growing fruit; you can imagine them growing golden candlesticks or tigers hanging by the tail."

Yet the fact that scientists don't wonder about why trees grow fruit, why rain falls from clouds, and other such facts of nature shows that they are not operating from the first principles that they vaunt. Chesterton draws a "sharp distinction between the science of mental relations, in which there really are laws, and the science of physical facts, in which there are no laws, but only weird repetitions."

No laws in nature? Chesterton is making a very bold claim indeed, yet one that we would do well to ponder.

Things don't happen because of some necessary law but because, well, they happen. The fact that the sun rises every morning is not because of some scientific necessity. It just happens day after day. We can predict it, but only because it did it yesterday and the day before. We will have no scientific reason to complain if it does not do so tomorrow. Yet scientists seem to "feel that because one incomprehensible thing constantly follows another incomprehensible thing, the two together somehow make up a comprehensible thing." Chesterton's point is that rain, sunshine, clouds, the earth, trees are all radically mysterious in and of themselves: science can only comprehend their relationship, such as the wind blowing the clouds, or the clouds dripping rain; but science cannot comprehend the things themselves.

"When we are asked why eggs turn into birds or fruits fall in autumn," Chesterton writes, "we must answer exactly as the fairy godmother would answer if Cinderella asked her why mice turned into horses or her clothes fell from her at twelve o'clock. We must answer that it is magic. It is not a law, for we do not understand its general formula. It is not a necessity, for although we can count on it happening practically, we have no right to say that it must happen." Chesterton protests scientific terms such as law, necessity, order, and tendency because, he argues "they assume an inner synthesis [in nature] which we do not possess." He prefers terms used in fairy-tale books such as charm, spell, and enchantment. "They express the arbitrariness of the fact and its mystery. A tree grows fruit because it is a magic tree. Water runs downhill because it is bewitched."

Chesterton then looks more closely at fairy tales and identifies what he playfully calls the Doctrine of Conditional Joy. "In a fairy tale," he observes, "an incom-

143

prehensible happiness rests upon an incomprehensible condition. A box is opened, and all evils fly out. A word is forgotten, and cities perish. A lamp is lit, and love flies away. A flower is plucked, and human lives are forfeited. An apple is eaten, and the hope of God is gone."

In one extended stretch of metaphor, Chesterton has linked those funny stories we were told in our youth with the biblical tale of the fall — Adam and Eve eating the apple, and mankind being doomed as a result. Chesterton's point is that religious truth may be incomprehensible to us, but it is no more so than the things we see and touch around us every day. The way for us to approach religious and temporal experience, Chesterton suggests, is not to walk around in a torpor, but rather to appreciate the mystery and wonder of it all, and then to start thinking about it. Here is where the intellect comes in.

Although many people view repetition in nature as a sign of the orderly and the rational, Chesterton says that "the mere repetition made the things rather more weird to me than more rational. It was as if, having seen a curiously shaped nose in the street and dismissed it as an accident, I had then seen six other noses of the same astonishing shape." To Chesterton life seemed like a conspiracy of bizarre accidents. "One elephant having a trunk was odd, but all elephants having trunks looked like a plot." What was going on here?

"The recurrences of the universe rose to the maddening rhythm of an incantation," says Chesterton, "and I began to see an idea. It is supposed that if a thing goes on repeating itself it is probably dead, a piece of clockwork." But in fact it could be the opposite. "It might be true that the sun rises regularly because he never gets tired of rising. A child kicks its legs rhythmically through excess, not absence, of life." Maybe it is true that "grown-up people are not strong enough to exult in monotony, but perhaps God is strong enough to exult in monotony . . . it may be that he has the eternal appetite of infancy." Nature, Chesterton suggests, may be nothing more than a "theatrical encore."

The moment Chesterton got to thinking in this admittedly bizarre and fanciful way, it occurred to him that not only were the everyday things and happenings of nature miraculous and wonderful, but these miracles were also willful: they represented something or someone's desire to have the tree grow fruit and the sun shine. Not only once, but again and again and again. "In short," Chesterton writes, "I had always believed that the world involved magic: now I thought that perhaps it involved a magician." The reasoning was simply that if there is a purpose, there must be a person behind it; "if there is a story, there is a story-teller."

Chesterton began with the notion that things were radically mysterious to man, not just the very odd things which we call miracles, but even the routine things which are in fact more astonishing and difficult to explain. But now he realizes that even though the universe must be a mystery for man it cannot be a mystery for its Maker. And there has to be a maker of something so large, complex and awesome. Man looks at little objects — pretty little clocks and nicely sculptured statues — and wonders who made them; he does not assume they simply made themselves, or existed for all time, or don't need a source at all. So why did so much of mankind start doubting that the universe needs a source?

For a silly reason, says Chesterton. Starting with Copernicus, man "popularized this contemptible notion that the size of the solar system ought to over-awe the spiritual dogma of man." Here Chesterton simplifies a bit. The medieval Christians based their understanding on the Ptolemaic universe with the earth at its center. When man learned that this was not the case, it was a tremendous blow to his psyche. It has spiritual ramifications because the fact that the earth was at the center of the universe was previously used to justify man as being the apple of God's eye. But now man seemed so small, so remote. If God existed, the question was raised, would he really care?

Chesterton is right that a geographical or astronomical finding such as this should not have dealt such a blow to the spiritual understanding. After all, he sensibly points out, "It is quite futile to argue that man is small compared to the cosmos, for man was always small compared to the nearest tree." So what if man is tiny, so what if the earth is on the margins of the universe? That fact, Chesterton maintains, says nothing about the true nature of man, about who made him, and why.

The philosophy that people who had lost their faith as Copernican discoveries developed was one that was profoundly hostile to free will. The materialists argued that there is nothing in the cosmos except material things; everything comes down to atoms whirling about mindlessly, which applies also to the human body and mind.

"In fairyland there had always been a real law, a law that could be broken, for the definition of a law is something that can be broken," Chesterton writes in *Orthodoxy*. "But the machinery of the [materialist] cosmic prison was something that could not be broken, for we ourselves were only part of its machinery. We were either unable to do things or we were destined to do them. The idea of the mystical condition quite disappeared; one can have neither the firmness of keeping laws nor the fun of breaking them."

146

After all, it is atoms that dictate everything; there is no will behind them telling them what to do. Such a universe may be large, Chesterton concedes, "but it is not free." Those who believe in free will, those who experience free will in their daily lives, must look elsewhere for an explanation of man.

The first part of *Orthodoxy* closes with a synthesis. Chesterton has rambled far, and his purple prose makes it seem that he has gone even further than he has. Now he must bring the reader home for a rest. "I felt in my bones," he writes, "first that this world does not explain itself. Second, I came to feel as if magic must have a meaning, and meaning must have someone to mean it. Third, I thought this purpose beautiful in its old design, in spite of its defects, such as dragons. Fourth, that the proper form of thanks to it is some form of humility and restraint: we should thank God for beer and burgundy by not drinking too much of them. We owed also an obedience to whatever made us. And last, and strangest, there came into my mind a vague and vast impression that in some way all good was a remnant to be stored and held sacred out of some primordial ruin." And all this time, concludes Chesterton, "I had not even thought of Christian theology."

From this luminous account Chesterton moves to a discussion of what exactly Christianity is and what its merits are as a religion. Chesterton says he began to discover Christianity by reading all the hostile accounts of it, from Huxley to Bradlaugh, and he discovered, he says, that Christianity was not only a "flaming vice," but it had "a mystical talent for combining vices which seemed inconsistent with each other. It was attacked on all sides and for all contradictory reasons."

Chesterton gives a series of examples. There were

147

those who said that Christianity is far too western, too Occidental; there were others who condemned its Oriental and mystical flavor. It was savaged for being too rationalistic; it was also attacked for being too mystical. There were those who said it focused too much on the next world; others insisted it was far too concerned with temporal pleasures such as grand cathedrals. Some condemned Christianity for preventing men, by morbid terror, from finding joy in the spontaneity of life, but another accusation was that Christianity comforted man with a fictitious providence and secured him from the terrors of real life. Christianity was scolded for its "naked and hungry habits" such as sackcloth and dried peas, observed Chesterton, but the next minute it was reproached for its pomp and ritualism, "its shrines of porphyry and its robes of gold." Christianity was also derided as too timid, monkish, and unmanly when its Gospel talked about "turning the other cheek"; but it was also blamed for fighting too much — for the Crusades, for the Inquisition.

What was Chesterton to make of this "mass of mad contradictions," as he calls them? "I did not conclude that the attack on Christianity was wrong," he writes. "Such hostile horrors might be combined in one thing, but that thing must be very strange and solitary." Chesterton comments that "such a paradox of evil rose to the stature of the supernatural. It was, indeed, almost as supernatural as the infallibility of the pope." Chesterton notes that, following this line of attack on Christianity, "the only explanation which immediately occurred to my mind was that Christianity did not come from heaven, but from hell. Really, if Jesus of Nazareth was not Christ, he must have been Antichrist."

Then, says Chesterton, "a strange thought struck me

like a still thunderbolt." Another explanation occurred to him. All these contradictory criticisms might point to one thing: Christianity might be the right shape, after all. The critical perspectives might be skewed. A man who is the right height might be viewed as abnormally tall by a dwarf and abnormally short by a giant; these comments would cast more light on the observer than on the observed. Perhaps, Chesterton thought, "this extraordinary thing is really the ordinary thing, the normal thing, the center."

Man's view of the Church may reflect not the Church's but his own deficiencies, Chesterton began to suspect. He realized that "modern man found the Church too simple where modern life is too complex; he found the Church too gorgeous exactly where modern life is too dingy." As he tested this against experience, Chesterton realized he was right: "the key fitted." Men attacked the spectacular robes and the poor meals of the monks, and yet "no man before modern man ever ate such elaborate dinners in such ugly clothes," notes Chesterton wryly. In a more serious vein, philosophers such as Swinburne expressed irritation with the unhappiness associated with Christianity, yet seemed even more irked at the happiness of Christians. "It was no longer a complication of diseases in Christianity," Chesterton saw, "but a complication of diseases in Swinburne. The restraint of the Christians saddened him because he was more hedonist than a healthy man should be. The faith of Christians angered him because he was more pessimist than a healthy man should be."

Next Chesterton criticizes the notion of the "virtuous pagan," the good man who doesn't think he needs religion. Taking a cue from the Greeks (specifically from Aristotle's doctrine of the mean), modern-day agnostics try to live good secular lives through maintaining a sort of balance. "The average agnostic would merely say that he was content with himself, but not insolently self-satisfied, that there were many better and many worse, that his deserts were limits, but he would see that he got them." Chesterton concedes that this is a "manly and rational position, but it is open to the objection: being a mixture of two things, it is a dilution." Put unkindly, it is a mushy and therefore uninteresting philosophy.

Christianity, by contrast, "separated the two ideas and then exaggerated them both. In one way man was to be haughtier than he had ever been before, in another way he was to be humbler than he had ever been before. Insofar as I am man, I am the chief of creatures. Insofar as I am a man, I am the chief of sinners." This breaks with Greek philosophy, which spoke of "men creeping on the earth, as if clinging to it. Now man was to tread on the earth as if to subdue it." Man had dominion over all God's creatures, as God said in Genesis. "Yet at the same time [Christianity] could hold a thought about the abject smallness of man that could only be expressed in fasting and fantastic submission, in the gray ashes of Saint Dominic and the white snows of Saint Bernard." Man, champion of earth, has also sinned in a way that cuts himself off from his Maker, God.

Thus Chesterton views Christianity as striking a balance between optimism and pessimism by allowing both free rein. "Let man say anything against himself short of blaspheming the original aim of all his being; let him call himself a fool and even a damned fool; but he must not say that fools are not worth saving."

Chesterton gives another example: charity. "A sensible pagan would say that there were some people one could forgive, and some one couldn't: a slave who stole wine could be laughed at; a slave who betrayed his bene-factor could be killed and cursed even after he was killed." Although this is rational, Chesterton argues that "it is a dilution: it leaves no place for a pure horror of in-justice . . . and it leaves no place for a mere tenderness for men as men," which is the definition of true charity.

So how does Christianity solve the problem? "It divided the crime from the criminal. The criminal we must forgive unto seventy times seven. The crime we must not forgive at all." This applies both to the slave who stole wine and to the slave who was treacherous. "It was not merely enough that slaves who stole wine in-spired partly anger and partly kindness. We must be much more angry with theft than before, and yet much kinder to thieves than before." So Christianity gives room "for wrath and love to run wild." This is the pur-pose of the order of Christianity, then, not to constrain emotion but to liberate it. To allow freedom.

Chesterton makes one final observation about the fine points of orthodoxy. Many laments have been echoed about the terrible wars and casualties about small items of theology, "the earthquakes of emotion about a gesture or word." But, says Chesterton, "it was only a matter of an inch, but an inch is everything when you are balanc-ing." Because Christianity is a "daring experiment" in conflicting emotion, a paradox which allows man to en-joy all aspects of life fully, to stretch out in all four direc-tions like the cross, it is important to maintain this "ir-regular equilibrium." Let one idea become too powerful and another will become too weak. "It is no flock of sheep the Christian shepherd is leading, but a herd of bulls and tigers, of terrible ideals and devouring doc-trines, each one of them strong enough to turn to a false religion and lay waste the world."

Hence the importance of doctrine and of order. "If some small mistake were made in doctrine, huge blunders might be made in human happiness." The Church has to be careful "if only that the world might be careless." This, then, for Chesterton is the "thrilling romance of orthodoxy." It is wrong to speak of orthodoxy as "something heavy, humdrum and safe," he says. "There never was anything so perilous or so exciting as orthodoxy." It is easy to be a heretic — just say anything that comes to mind — but it is difficult to stay within the wild and yet precise parameters of orthodoxy. "It is always simple to fall," notes Chesterton; "there is an infinity of angles at which one falls; only one at which one stands." To fall into one of the fads of modern philosophy is obvious and tame, he concludes, "but to have avoided them is one whirling adventure; and in my vision the heavenly chariot flies thundering through the ages, the dull heresies sprawling and prostrate, the wild truth reeling but erect."

With this brilliant image, *Orthodoxy* comes to its end. But for Chesterton true orthodoxy was yet to come. He followed the instruction of his writings, pushing the logic further and further. Finally, on July 30, 1922, Chesterton converted to Roman Catholicism. His wife followed him four years later. Chesterton spent the rest of his life as a famous lecturer and writer. He produced three theological studies, *St. Francis of Assisi, The Everlasting Man*, and *The Dumb Ox* (a biography of Thomas Aquinas), all of which are worth reading.

G.K. Chesterton died in Beaconsfield on June 14, 1936. Throughout his life he described himself only as a journalist. But he left behind great accomplishments as a dramatist, novelist, biographer, poet, literary commentator, and most important of all, Christian apologist.

merton's

seven storey mountain

NAMING a recent classic is a difficult task. Samuel Johnson's test of a truly great work was that it should pass the test of time as it accrued the appreciation of wise men of several generations. Otherwise, Johnson worried, books that were merely fashionable or limited in their appeal could be mistaken for classics. Of Thomas Merton's *Seven Storey Mountain* it may be said that, although written in 1948, its place is secure in history. Already it has been compared to Saint Augustine's *Confessions*, and by so careful and authoritative a figure as Bishop Fulton Sheen.

When the *Seven Storey Mountain* was published, it shook the Catholic world, drew peering and somewhat amazed attention from the outside, and established an obscure Trappist monk as a beacon for modern-day people interested in the spiritual experience.

Nowadays we are tempted to discount spiritual experience. Some of us are even skeptical about whether our ancestors in the faith truly had such experiences; we wonder if they merely confused the scientific unknown with the miraculous. Merton's book is not about miracles, in the sense of natural laws being distorted; rather, it is about the miracle of one man, through God's grace, transcending his thoroughly modern and even sophisticated surroundings and committing himself to a medieval-style monastery, "the four walls of my newfound freedom," he says.

Like most great Catholic works the *Seven Storey Mountain* is the odyssey of the anguished soul to its Creator. The difference is that until very recently the monastic life was quite a logical route for many young people; certainly it was not viewed as unusual or bizarre. Merton is one who wrenched himself from twentieth-century American life to seek spiritual calm in the wilderness.

"On the last day of January 1915, under the sign of the Water Bearer, in a year of a great war, and down in the shadow of some French mountains on the borders of Spain, I came into the world." Thus the book begins. Young Thomas Merton's parents were "in the world and not of it — not because they were saints, but in a different way: because they were artists." They viewed themselves, and their son, as spectators of, not participants in, life's drama. They were not religious believers, so Merton received no religious training. Merton comments that his parents regarded religious "superstition" as too base for the elevated artistic sensibility. Yet Merton's father was not anti-religious; "his vision was religious and clean, and therefore his paintings were without decoration or superfluous comment, since a religious man respects the power of God's creation to bear witness for itself," Merton writes.

From an early age young Thomas developed a love of reading. He had a spell where he was enchanted by the Greek myths, he writes, "and it was from them that I unconsciously built up the vague fragments of a religion and of a philosophy, which remained hidden and implicit in my acts, and which in due time were to assert themselves." Here Merton is in the tradition of so many Catholic thinkers who were influenced by the Greeks and Romans, and even assimilated elements of ancient philosophy into their Christian synthesis.

Merton moved around quite a lot in his youth. For a time he lived with his grandmother in Douglaston, New York. His mother got cancer and wrote Thomas saying that she was about to die and might never see him again. But even in that moment of what would normally be a crisis in a person's life — the imminent death of one's mother — "prayer did not occur to me," Merton writes. It was only twenty years later, when he became a Catholic, that he prayed for his mother.

From his father Merton acquired a "subconscious aversion" to Catholicism. "I did not know precisely what the word meant. It only conveyed a kind of cold and unpleasant feeling." Later, when Merton purchased and read *The Spirit of Medieval Philosophy* by the distinguished Catholic writer Étienne Gilson, a book that would greatly influence his life, Merton admits he never would have bought it if he had known it carried a *nihil obstat* and an *imprimatur*, thereby "having the Vatican's approval," no less.

Visiting Cazals in France, Merton was impressed by the grandeur of the churches, especially St. Antonin's Church. It was a partly broken edifice, still bearing the wounds of the religious wars of the past. "Even now, however, the church dominated the town, and each noon and evening sent forth the Angelus bells over the brown, ancient tiled roofs reminding the people of the Mother of God who watched over them."

In a passionate aside Merton remarks, "I thought

churches were simply places where people got together and sang a few hymns. And yet now I tell you, you who are now what I once was, unbelievers, it is that sacrament, and that alone, the Christ living in our midst, and sacrificed by us, and for us and with us, in the clean and perpetual sacrifice, it is he alone who holds our world together, and keeps us all from being poured headlong and immediately into the pit of eternal destruction. There is a power that goes forth from that sacrament, a power of light and truth, even into the hearts of those who have heard nothing of him [that is, Christ] and seem to be incapable of belief."

Passages like this appear frequently in the *Seven Storey Mountain*. They represent the new Merton, the converted Merton, interrupting his spiritual recollection with an outburst of love of God and conviction. The effect of these passages is not to slow the pace of the narrative but to enrich it, however, because they reinforce in the reader's mind the depth of Merton's conviction. He is impatient; he cannot even tell the story of his own unbelief without reminding the reader: I was wrong then, I was a fool, can't you see?

What revolted Merton about religion in Europe was its artificiality. "The most shocking thing about France is the corruption of French spirituality into flippancy and cynicism; of French intelligence into sophistry; of French dignity and refinement into petty vanity and theatrical self-display; of French charity into fleshly concupiscence, and of French faith into sentimentality or puerile atheism." Merton makes this as a secular observation; even as a nonbeliever he expects to see a difference in French Catholics, and finds little.

While staying with the Privat family in Paris, however, he discovered a couple truly devoted to Christ and the Catholic faith. Their quiet conviction irritated Merton, "so I began to justify Protestantism as best I could. . . . I gave the argument that every religion was good, they all led to God, only in different ways, and every man should go according to his own conscience." They did not, however, answer him with argument but simply maintained, *"Mais c'est impossible."* Merton comments, "It was a terrible, a frightening, a very humiliating thing to feel all their silence and peacefulness and strength turned against me, accusing me of being estranged from them, isolated from their security, cut off from their protection and from the strength of their inner life by my own fault."

But from the Privats Merton discovered that there are people who believe in the one faith that is true, and in retrospect, he observes, "Who knows how much I owe those two wonderful people?" Certainly many graces due to their prayers, and perhaps ultimately the grace of his conversion, Merton tells us.

Attending the Oakham private school in the English Midlands, Merton went through a "religious phase," he writes. Immediately he turns on this sort of self-characterization that we hear so often: "If the impulse to worship God and to adore him in truth by the goodness and order of our own lives is nothing more than a transitory and emotional thing, that is our own fault. It is so only because we make it so, and because we take what is substantially a deep and powerful and lasting moral impetus, supernatural in its origin and in its direction, and reduce it to the level of our own weak and unstable and futile fancies and desires."

His brief religious flirtation was cut short by revulsion to what he calls the English "class religion," an Anglicanism without doctrinal unity or mystical bond but rather a vague glue holding together "a big, sweet complex of subjective dispositions regarding the English countryside, old castles and cottages, games of cricket in the summer afternoons, tea parties on the Thames . . . and all those other things the mere thought of which produces a kind of warm and inexpressible ache" in the upper-class British heart.

What Merton regards as this "manifest pretense" was best embodied in his school chaplain at Oakham, who taught that charity in the Bible was just another term for "being a gentleman." One should peruse Saint Paul and simply replace the word gentleman for the word charity, this man maintained.

"The boys listened tolerantly to these thoughts," Merton comments. "But I think Saint Peter and the twelve apostles would have been rather surprised at the concept that Christ had been scourged and beaten by soldiers, cursed and crowned with thorns and subjected to unutterable contempt and finally nailed to the cross and left to bleed to death in order that we might all become gentlemen."

One can see that Merton's diversions are often the most succulent part of his book; they represent a mature intellect and a mature emotion reflecting upon an unwiser period in Merton's life, among like-minded fellow students and teachers.

To revive a youthful passion for Greek, Merton enrolled in courses on the classics. But this time he was repulsed. "After a couple of months, I got to a state where phrases like The Good, The True, and The Beautiful filled me with a kind of suppressed indignation because they stood for the big sin of Platonism: the reduction of all reality to the level of pure abstraction." Merton realized the parallel between classical abstractions and high-church English theology, both of which celebrated "culture" but did nothing for the spirit.

Immersed in philosophy, Merton learned about Descartes and his proof for God's existence. Taking nothing for granted, Descartes began with the fact that he doubted. Because he doubted, he knew he was thinking. "I think, therefore I am," he maintained. And from Descartes' idea of God he reasoned, similarly, that God must exist as well. But this proof "never convinced me then or at any other time," says Merton. "There are much better proofs for the existence of God than that one."

Merton found that the experience of wafting from one philosophy to another, considering and then rejecting each, was instilling in him a deep skepticism and relativism. His father's untimely death halted this drift, but in a few months even that was a blurred memory. "The hard crust of my soul had finally squeezed out all the last traces of religion that had ever been in it. There was no room for any God in that empty temple full of dust and rubbish which I was now so jealously guarding against all intruders, in order to devote it to the worship of my own stupid will." In following his own base emotions all the way, "I became the complete twentieth-century man," writes Merton.

The poetry of William Blake, on whom Merton was writing his master's thesis, helped revive the lost spiritualism in Merton's soul. It intrigued Merton to discover that Blake hated Rousseau and Voltaire: "Blake was a revolutionary, and yet he detested the greatest and most typical revolutionaries of his time, and declared himself opposed without compromise to people who, as I thought, seemed to exemplify some of his own most characteristic ideals." But soon Merton recognized that Blake's rebellion, "for all its strange heterodoxies, was fundamentally the rebellion of the saints. . . . He simply could not stand false piety and religiosity, in which the love of God was stamped out of the souls of men by formalism and conventions, without any charity, without the light and life of a faith that brings man face to face with God."

There was much that was bizarre and heretical in Blake, and yet Merton found that his "desire of God was so intense and irresistible that it condemned, with all its might, all the hypocrisy and petty sensuality and skepticism and materialism which trivial minds set up as impassable barriers between God and the souls of men." In other words Blake's errors, though reprehensible in themselves, flowed from a heart bursting with urgency in its desire to reach God.

In his late teens Merton got blood poisoning, had to be hospitalized, and was on the verge of death. Just as when his mother was very ill, he did not even bother to pray. Even when others recited the Apostles' Creed in his presence, Merton says he kept his lips tightly shut. "I thought I believed in nothing," Merton remembers. But "actually I had only exchanged a certain faith, faith in God, for a vague uncertain faith in the opinions and authority of men and pamphlets and newspapers — wavering and contradictory opinions which I did not even clearly understand."

A visit to Rome during the holidays brought him face to face with the earthly abode of Christianity, at least early Christianity. Young Merton stood awestruck before St. Peter's Basilica, the tombs of the martyrs, the great statues in the churches. "Now for the first time in my life I began to find out something of the man called Christ." What some Protestants disdainfully call idols helped Merton imagine Christ's grandeur, although he did not confuse the marble with the spiritual entity they were intended to point to and represent.

The prelude to Merton's conversion was his reading of some poems by D.H. Lawrence on the four evangelists. "I became so disgusted with their falseness and futility that I threw down the book and began to ask myself why I was wasting my time with a man of such unimportance as this. For it was evident that he had more or less completely failed to grasp the true meaning of the New Testament, which he had perverted in the interests of a personal and home-made religion of his own which was not only fanciful, but full of unearthly seeds, all ready to break forth into hideous plants like those that were germinating in Germany's unweeded garden, in the dank weather of Nazism."

Merton swapped Lawrence for the Gospels he was trying to denigrate, and his love for the churches of Rome grew from day to day. "Soon I was no longer visiting them merely for the art. There was something else that attracted me: a kind of interior peace." One night Merton dreamed that his dead father was standing in front of him and touched him. "The whole thing passed in a flash, but in that flash, instantly, I was overwhelmed with a sudden and profound insight into the misery and corruption of my own soul. . . . My whole being rose up in revolt against what was within me, and my soul desired escape and liberation and freedom from all this with an intensity and an urgency unlike anything I had ever known before. And now I think for the first time in my whole life I began to pray — praying not with my lips and my intellect and my imagination but praying out of the very roots of my life and of my being, and praying to the God I had never known, to reach down toward me out of his darkness and to help me to get free of the thousand terrible things that held my will in their slavery."

Self-conscious and embarrassed, Merton stumbled to a Catholic church the next day, and "after that I walked out into the open, feeling as if I had been reborn." This account by Merton of his religious conversion is about as authentic and persuasive as any that has been written. And yet the soul does not give in to God's beckoning without a fight. "There is no point in telling all the details of how this real but temporary religious fervor cooled down and disappeared," Merton writes with scarcely concealed disgust at himself and almost a resignation over the obstinacy of the human mind.

Back in New York, Merton attended services at the Mount Zion church where he was "very irritated, and my own pride increased the irritation and complicated it." It was not until Merton returned to Europe to attend Cambridge, and immersed himself in spiritual reading — Dante's *Divine Comedy*, Thomas à Kempis's *Imitation of Christ* — that he caught new glimpses of God's love. Otherwise everything was negative. Merton realized that he was in a spiritual quandary, but "the mere realization of one's own unhappiness is not salvation: it may be the occasion of salvation, or it may be the door to a deeper pit in hell."

It was a prelude to a conversion, but the wrong kind — Merton found himself becoming a Communist. "I had read some books about Soviet Russia, how all the factories were working overtime, and everyone wore great big smiles on their faces, welcoming Russian aviators on their return from polar nights, bearing the boughs of trees in their hands. . . . I also had the myth that Soviet Russia was the friend of all the arts, and the only place where true art could find a refuge in a world of bourgeois ugliness." In fact, Merton soon realized that his attraction to Communism was mainly a pretext to blame the invidious economic forces in society, not himself, for his own unhappiness. It was important for society to change, perhaps, but it was more important for Merton to change.

From Cambridge it was back to Columbia University in New York for Merton. By now it is beginning to seem like we have a perpetual student on our hands. Merton's restless intellect and his restless heart kept him searching for answers in the halls of academe, it appears. Yet he was not making much progress. "I had refused to pay attention to the moral laws upon which all our vitality and sanity depend, and so now I was reduced to the condition of a silly old woman, worrying about a lot of imaginary rules of health, standards of food-value, and a thousand minute details of conduct that were in themselves completely ridiculous and stupid, and yet which haunted me with terrific sanctions."

Fortunately this time Merton's despair and defeat were the occasion of his rescue. His chapter "With a Great Price" chronicles an event the reader has been waiting for with great anticipation, Merton's true conversion. "There is a paradox that lies in the very heart of human existence," this chapter begins. "It must be apprehended before any lasting happiness is possible in the soul of man. The paradox is this: man's nature, by itself, can do little or nothing to settle his most important problems. If we follow nothing but our natures, our own philosophies, our own level of ethics, we will end up in hell."

Here we get to the heart of Merton's philosophy. Indeed it is wrong to call it his philosophy because, as he insists, he didn't come up with it. Essentially it is a philosophy of surrender to God's will, a willingness to acquiesce in God's philosophy or plan, whatever it is. "God created man with a soul that was made not to bring itself a perfection in its own order, but to be perfected by him [that is, the Creator] in an order infinitely beyond the reach of human powers," Merton writes.

Two writers — Étienne Gilson and Aldous Huxley — solidified Merton's developing Christian commitment. In Gilson's works Merton "discovered an entirely new concept of God — a concept which showed me at once that the belief of Catholics was by no means the vague and superstitious hangover from an unscientific age that I had believed it to be. On the contrary, here was a notion of God that was at the same time deep, precise, simple, and accurate and, what is more, charged with implications that I could only dimly appreciate, with my lack of philosophical training." Gilson was, of course, the famous scholar of Thomas Aquinas. What Merton was startled by was the Thomistic rendition of God as Being itself — not abstract Being but actual Being, not caused by anything else, existing only in virtue of itself. *Ergo sum qui sum:* God's nature is "to be."

From Huxley's book *Ends and Means* Merton learned that "we cannot use evil means to attain a good end." Huxley argues that although man cherishes decent ends, the means he uses to achieve them — war, violence, reprisals, greed — deny the very ideals of his objective. "The main problem," comments Merton, "is to fight our way free from subjection to this more or less inferior element, man's interior urges, and to reassert the dominance of our mind and our will: to vindicate for these faculties, for the spirit as a whole, freedom of action. . . . And the big conclusion from all this was that we must practice prayer and asceticism."

Prayer and asceticism. "The very thought was a

complete revolution in my mind," writes Merton. "These things had never succeeded in giving me anything but gooseflesh." But now Merton was beginning to see that self-denial was "not something absolute, sought for its own sake, but it was a freeing of our real selves, a liberation of the spirit from limits and bonds that are intolerable, suicidal. . . . Not only that, once the spirit is free and returned to its own element, it is not alone there: it can find the absolute and perfect Spirit, God. It can enter into union with him, and what is more this union is not something metaphorical, but it is a matter of real experience."

Merton discovered that one does not have to wait until the afterlife for one's spirit to find God. In fact, then it might be too late. Through self-sacrifice, the gradual extirpation of the excess of human desire, man could emancipate his spirit for an earthly communion with God's spirit. This would be a fitting rehearsal for the afterlife.

Through some friends Merton met a Hindu sage, Bramachari, whom he found a wise and witty companion. Merton was surprised when Bramachari did not direct him to Oriental texts for mysticism. "You should read Saint Augustine's *Confessions* and the *Imitation of Christ*," he advised. Merton found it ironic that he had turned, spontaneously, to the east for spirituality and mysticism, ignoring the mysticism in his own Christian tradition. "Now I was told that I ought to turn to the Christian tradition, to Saint Augustine, and told by a Hindu monk" no less.

Merton's conversion was now being consummated, and it was not the early flush, the adolescent acquiescence, temporary and soon overwhelmed by desires of the mind and the heart. This time it was a genuine change of heart and soul, a conversion intellectual as well as emotional. Merton movingly describes his First Communion on November 16, 1938. The confession before in which "I tore out all the sins by their roots, like teeth," and then the celestial experience, receiving the sacrament, after which Merton emerged, quiet but feeling that "heaven was entirely mine."

Shortly after, the "big defect in his spiritual life" — his lack of devotion to the Virgin Mary — was overcome. "People do not realize the tremendous power of the Blessed Virgin," Merton writes. "Through her hands all graces come because God has willed that she thus participate in his work for the salvation of men." No longer was our Lady a "beautiful myth" to Merton. She was a very real intercessor for man to Christ.

In the late 1930s the world was getting ready for war. On Merton's way to Mass one day, in 1939, he heard that the Nazis were bombing Warsaw and attacking by blitzkrieg. Soon the savagery mounted into a full-scale European war. Yet, in the middle of this, "an idea came to me," writes Merton, "an idea that was startling enough and momentous enough" to be disbelieved. While he was sitting on the floor playing records and eating breakfast, Merton turned to his roommate and said, "I am going to become a priest."

It was not a thing of passion or fancy, Merton says. "It was a strong and sweet and deep and insistent attraction that suddenly made itself felt, but not as a movement of appetite. It was something in the order of conscience, a new and profound and clear sense that this is what I really ought to do."

His friend Dan Walsh at first thought he was fooling. But when he was convinced of Merton's sincerity, he recommended that Merton visit a Trappist monastery. Its members were the Order of Cistercians, the Cistercians of the Strict Observance. No ordinary monks they. Even their name conjured up fearful images of reclusiveness. And their common name, the Trappists, was equally mysterious to Merton. He found out from Walsh that the Trappists hung large signs outside their monasteries warning women not to enter on pain of excommunication; they required silence and meditation most of the time, with breaks only for Mass and confession. Merton shivered.

Yet when he visited the Trappists, when he made retreats with them, when he discovered what they were really like, Merton realized "what wonderful happiness there still was in the world. There were still men on this miserable, noisy, cruel earth who tasted the marvelous joy of silence and solitude, who dwelt in forgotten mountain cells, in secluded monasteries. They were free from the burden of the flesh's tyranny. They were poor, they had nothing, and therefore they were free and possessed everything, and everything they touched struck of something of the fire of divinity. And they worked with their hands, silently plowing and harrowing the earth, and sowing seed in obscurity, and reaping their small harvests to feed themselves and the other poor. They had found Christ, and they knew the power of living and working with him and in him."

Merton writes, "If happiness were merely a matter of natural gifts, I would never have entered a Trappist monastery when I came to the age of a man." But he did, in Kentucky in December 1941, and the *Seven Storey Mountain* is a powerful account of how he came to that decision.

Merton lived out his last years as a Cistercian monk. He took the name of Frater M. Louis and discovered in that new person, he says, his true identity. For years people across the world corresponded with Merton, whose only interaction with the outside world was his mail. But through his inspiring letters he conveyed something of the love and wisdom he secured through the isolated life to people living in noise and clutter on the outside.